by Ryan Lindbuchler

Luzerne County Historical Society, Wilkes-Barre, PA

Gone But Not Forgotten
Civil War Veterans of Northeastern Pennsylvania

by Ryan L. Lindbuchler

Production:
Produced in cooperation with VidaWorks

Christopher J. Vida, Proprietor

Copyright ©2001 by Ryan L. Lindbuchler
Published by the Luzerne County Historical Society.
All rights reserved, including the right of reproduction in whole or in part in any form.

Printed in the United States of America.
Offset Paperback Mfrs., Inc.
P.O. Box N, 101 Memorial Highway
Dallas, PA 18612

ISBN 0-937537-11-X

Table of Contents

Foreword 2

Acknowledgements 4

Introduction 5

Methodology 6

Civil War Army Structure 9

Directory of Cemeteries 10

Biographies Index 14

Biographies 15-161

Regimental Sketches 162-189

Bibliography 190

Brian C. Pohanka is a long-time Civil War reenactor, historian, and author. He has served several years as a researcher and writer for Time-Life Books. He is the author of *Distant Thunder: A Photographic Essay on the American Civil War*, and has written several articles and other works on American military history. He also has served as a historical consultant for the television documentary series called *Civil War Journal*, and the motion picture *Glory*. He is an accomplished public speaker and is very active in battlefield conservation.

Ryan Lindbuchler

Detail of the gravestone of Private Joseph Frey, Company F, 97th Pennsylvania Volunteer Infantry, Tunkhannock Cemetery Credit: Kristen Lindbuchler photo

FOREWORD

In the last decades of his long and productive career, Supreme Court Justice Oliver Wendell Holmes, a thrice-wounded veteran of the Civil War, would often go to Arlington National Cemetery to pay his respects to the thousands of unknown Federal soldiers who rest in that Hallowed ground. On one such visit, as he stood beside the mass grave of Union dead behind Arlington House, Holmes remarked to his secretary, "Can you imagine a greater gift than that? You not only gave your life but your identity as well….They gave their all. They gave their very names."

Justice Holmes had been one of that mighty host of volunteers. He had shared their hardships and witnessed their valor. He had seen dear friends die, torn with bullet and shell, or struck down by the ravages of disease. And their memories were so real to him as to be nearly tangible.

Those who went forth to battle in our nation's bloodiest conflict were endowed with patriotic devotion to country, and an ardor born of their belief in something greater than self, more enduring than life. Time and again, elbow to elbow and rank upon rank, they marched up into the face of death with bravery and idealism beyond the power of words to express. And for many tens of thousands, their fate was a shallow and anonymous grave, or a burial trench in which the dead were aligned, as they had been in regimental formation, beside their fallen comrades.

Fortunate were those families whose slain loved ones were returned to them, to be laid to rest in the farmstead plot, the village churchyard, or town cemetery. And in time, those veterans who had passed through the fires of that terrible war joined them there, in that last bivouac. A stone of marble or of granite marked their place, graven with words of honor and remembrance. Those monuments were not only tokens of familial love, but of national honor. As General Joshua Chamberlain put it, "We wish to be remembered. Willing to die, we are not willing to be forgotten."

Sadly, with the passage of time, many of those stones have become so worn and eroded by the elements that their inscriptions are entirely lost, or nearly illegible. Criminal vandalism and the thoughtless chaos of urban sprawl have also taken a toll, while the financial decline of once profitable cemeteries has seen manicured lawns and landscaped memorials turn to impenetrable jungles of riotous vegetation and toppled, shattered monuments.

Thus, tragically, many a Civil War veteran whose identity was preserved is now another "unknown soldier." And with that annihilation of name and of honor we lose something as a country and a people. They served, they gave, they died --- but all too often they are forgotten.

Those of us who do honor and remember can be thankful for the hard work and devotion of Ryan Lindbuchler, whose tireless, decades-long effort to record the burial places of Pennsylvania Civil War soldiers is represented in this volume. A project that began when the author was 15 years old has succeeded in preserving for the future the gravesites and the names of thousands of volunteers from the Keystone State who might otherwise have passed into oblivion. The daunting magnitude of Lindbuchler's task was matched by his persistence in seeing the work to fruition. And the information recorded here, often salvaged from the brink of dissolution, has an importance beyond that of paying deserved respect to the warriors of the Union.

Recent years have witnessed a burgeoning interest in genealogy, as families quest for their roots, tracing the invariably fascinating stories of their ancestors' experiences, men and women whose lives were interwoven with the fate of the American Republic. Exalted or humble, famous or obscure, those lives and those experiences serve to remind us that history truly is biography, and that each of us has a personal connection to the drama of the past.

The task of the genealogist has been greatly facilitated by an increased availability of archival resources, the remarkable growth of the Internet playing a major role in that regard. Census records, military service and pension files, registers of wills and legal transactions, immigration and naturalization papers ---all of these sources have emerged from dusty obscurity to further the efforts of the family researcher.

As anyone who has ever undertaken that genealogical exploration knows, cemeteries are a potential gold mine of ancestral data. When they exist, housed in cemetery offices, the ledger books containing records of burials offer an invaluable research tool. But the tombstones themselves often have a story to tell. Names, dates of birth and death, and epitaphs that are frequently biographical as well as sentimental tributes to deceased loved ones, provide the genealogist or historian with information that might not otherwise be discovered. Moreover, as we stand at their graves, we sense a bond to those we never knew --- a heartfelt empathy that transcends the ages.

This volume is thus not only a stirring tribute to those who fought in our great and tragic Civil War, but also a significant contribution to the genealogical record. Hopefully others, throughout our country, will be inspired to undertake their own quest to salvage the tombstone inscriptions of the Union or Confederate veterans interred in their region. I do not doubt that thanks to Ryan Lindbuchler's diligence and devotion, descendants of these soldiers will not only learn of their ancestors' military service, but be able to pay homage at the gravesides of selfless heroes who are family.

They were willing to die, and we will not forget them.

Brian C. Pohanka
Alexandria, Virginia
June 22, 2001

Acknowledgments

I would like to thank the many people who assisted with the research and support that made this book possible. First, I would like to thank Thomas Mooney, genealogy column writer/researcher for the Times Leader newspaper, and Jeff Frank, librarian/archivist for the Luzerne County Historical Society. They assisted me in gaining the needed information for many of the biographies that appear in this book. Also, I would like to thank Joe Long and Bob Shafer of the Scranton Sons of Union Veterans, Post 8, for all their help, especially in the collection of gravesites in Lackawanna County and their generosity in providing many of the photographs included in this work.

I would also like to thank Ted Dombroski, Scott Kuchta, and Dennis Rightmire, who were of great help in performing many foot searches in area cemeteries. Without their support, many cemeteries would have been omitted from this book. All three men and I are members of Company K, 81st Pennsylvania Volunteer Infantry Regiment, a Civil War reenactment unit based in Luzerne County.

Next, I would like to thank Charles McHugh Jr. of the Carbon County Veterans Affairs office and Michael Meehan, of the Luzerne County Veterans Affairs office. Both men advised me on the best way of using available county records to document grave locations and provided much encouragement for me during my searches. Also, I would like to acknowledge the photography of my sister, Kristen Lindbuchler, who took many of the beautiful photos included in this work.

Also, I would like to thank the board of directors of the Luzerne County Historical Society, especially Robert Janosov, Professor of History, Luzerne County Community College, whose help in planning and editing was invaluable in the publication of this book. I would also like to thank board president Larry Newman, past president John Orlandini, and society director Jesse Teitelbaum for believing in the preservation of the heritage and history of northeastern and central Pennsylvania. Only with their support and the financial backing of the Society was this book made possible.

Many thanks to Dr. Sheldon Spear, Professor Emeritus, LCCC; John Robert Kelleher, Professor Emeritus, LCCC; Daniel Stout, Professor of Humanities, LCCC; Stephen B. Killian, Esquire; and Sarah Carr for assisting with the editing of this book.

Finally, I would like to thank my wife, Anita, and our two boys, Ryan and Erik. Many a night and day I was engaged in the research required by this book, and missed out on time spent with them. To my parents, I would like to say thank you for instilling in me a feeling of pride, appreciation, and love of history that has been in my blood since I can remember. To all my family and friends, thank you for your love and support.

INTRODUCTION

The names of approximately 9,000 Civil War veterans located in 196 cemeteries throughout northeastern and central Pennsylvania are contained in this work. These veterans fought in the worst type of war that a nation can engage in: a civil war. The American Civil War was fought between the years 1861 and 1865 and claimed the lives of more than 600,000 Americans, exceeding the number killed for all other American wars combined.

Northeastern and central Pennsylvania responded to the call for volunteers by president Abraham Lincoln in 1861 and provided many men for the ranks. By 1865, Pennsylvania had raised about 215 regiments for the Union numbering about 338,000 men, second only to the state of New York. Many who left never returned, and those who survived bore the scars of war, both physically and psychologically. Some veterans who returned to the area became well-known and highly respected civic and social leaders. Others went back to their normal everyday lives as American citizens, feeling a great sense of pride in what their generation had accomplished, the Union had been preserved.

This work is an attempt to preserve their memory for our generation and those to come. Our local cemeteries are memorials to these men and women. The natural elements, vandals, and lack of upkeep have destroyed many of these last memorials. While walking through many cemeteries, I have noted numerous stones obliterated by these factors. This is not acceptable. The lists contained on this CD ROM will be a guarantee that the names, deeds, personalities, and heroics will endure the test of time. Their accomplishments will be preserved and give us pride and a patriotic feeling as citizens of this great nation.

The main section of this work contains cemetery lists. These lists contain names, ranks, regiments, companies, birth and death dates, and comments on individual soldiers, sailors, and marines. The second part of this work contains lists of veterans of local regiments and their final resting-places. A brief regimental history of local regiments has been added to aid the reader in understanding the experiences of these veterans. Information on specific battles mentioned can easily be located in various sources on Civil War military history. In the printed book, short biographies of several local veterans, rich and poor, appear. Photographs of these men and their tombstones are included whenever possible. Also included are photos of several interesting headstones found in local cemeteries.

It may seem a bit morbid, but I encourage readers to get out to your local cemeteries, take a slow walk, and just observe. Our cemeteries contain beautiful and intricate memorials to our ancestors. If a personality in this book interests you, do not hesitate to search for his or her final resting-place. Many times I have stood in awe as I discovered the grave of a brave soldier that I had read about and admired in the past. Perhaps if you are searching for a long-lost ancestor, his name may appear and you may be able to locate his grave. Northeastern and central Pennsylvania is not without history, it is rich.

Methodology

When I began this mammoth task, I had to adopt a general methodology to keep the listings relatively accurate and complete. The most basic part of my methodology is the cemetery walk-through. Upon finding the cemetery, which is a challenge in itself in some cases, I would walk down each row of graves observing and recording. First, I would note United States government stones. These stones make collecting names an easy task because name, company, regiment, and sometimes birth and death dates are engraved on the stone itself. However, by no means does every Civil War veteran have a government issue stone. I have found only about one third have these stones. Therefore, I had to include the observance of ALL stones in my search.

I would observe the birth and death years of the individual on each and every civilian stone. If the year of birth is no later than 1848 and no earlier than 1805, that man was considered in the right age range for military service between 1861 and 1865. Obviously, death dates are also important. If the man had died before the year 1861, he was not a veteran of that war.

The most frustrating aspect of this methodology is inaccuracy and incompleteness. Some stones are too worn to be read, others are broken, and some are nearly completely buried in the earth. There is nothing more aggravating than knowing that you have a veteran lying before you and you cannot read his stone to identify him and his regiment. Incompleteness is another nagging problem. No matter how well I thought I had a cemetery completed, there were always more veterans there that I somehow missed while recording. Friends who have assisted me with walk-throughs have, on occasion, covered the same cemetery on his own, and we found that we had some different names when notes were compared.

In order to address this incompleteness, the second part of my methodology had to be created. In order to gain a more complete listing of these veterans, other sources besides the cemeteries had to be drawn from. I found these sources in periodicals of the late 19th century and early 20th century. Because of the formation of veterans organizations such as the G.A.R. (Grand Army of the Republic) and the Sons of Union Veterans following the Civil War, much attention was given to veteran burials in newspapers. By consulting these periodicals in local historical societies, valuable knowledge was gained. There are burial books that were kept by G.A.R. members at their posts that can be helpful, but these books are often incomplete and hard to locate. In addition to these sources, there are several local historians who have compiled lists of this nature that can be used. Local Veterans' Affairs divisions of county governments have also been of great assistance because some hold listings of veteran burials that were compiled in the early part of the 20th century.

Once a list of names for a cemetery is in hand, the third portion of my methodology comes into play. Information recorded from government stones is for the most part complete and needs no further research, unless a stone has been worn away or broken and only partial information was recovered. The names recorded from civilian stones obviously need research. My first course of action would be to take the name in question and look it up in a set of books entitled

<u>History of Pennsylvania Volunteers</u>. This set of books was written by Samuel Bates in the latter part of the 19th century and is a listing of volunteers from the state of Pennsylvania who served during the Civil War. This set is essential to identifying possible veterans but is sometimes inaccurate and incomplete.

If Bates lists several references for a given name, each name is studied, taking note of: what county of the state that regiment and company was recruited from; possible death date; and comparisons between the possible regiment and the regiments found on government stones located in the cemetery being studied. If there are over five possible identifications, the person being researched is eliminated. In short, if there are less than five identifications on hand in Bates, a hypothesis (educated guess) is made, selecting the most likely candidate. Unfortunately, I did not have the resources to cross reference names that did not appear in Bates with lists from other states. I am positive that some names that were eliminated served for other states.

Once the name, regiment, and company are identified, each unit (by company) is cross-referenced with information contained in the book, <u>Advance the Colors!</u>, by Richard Sauers. This two-volume set lists each and every company raised within the Commonwealth and gives the nicknames of each, along with the county it was raised in. This information was included in my study as an interesting contrast between companies and regiments. I applaud Mr. Sauers on this book, as it is an indispensable resource to any Civil War historian.

In choosing which cemeteries I would analyze, I determined that I would exhaustively study Luzerne and Lackawanna Counties, and branch out to counties that are located adjacent to these two counties. Therefore, the majority of cemeteries in this book are located in Luzerne and Lackawanna Counties. However, I extended my search to include most of Carbon County, and the cemeteries from major cities that are located in surrounding counties, close to the Luzerne and Lackawanna County borders. **<u>Some</u>** of these include cemeteries in Bloomsburg, Pottsville, and Factoryville. In short, this book is a study of most of the cemeteries located in northeastern Pennsylvania.

Research of this type is not an exact science. There may be errors that become apparent. Please feel free to contact me or the Luzerne County Historical Society (the new name of the Wyoming Historical and Geological Society) with any corrections that may be necessary. With that, I present you with the following lists and short biographies of Civil War veterans in an attempt to preserve their names and sacrifices for future generations.

Notes

In order to prevent confusion the following list was created to assist the reader.

WIA = wounded in action	MW = mortally wounded
KIA = killed in action	POW = prisoner of war
Pvt. = Private	Cpl. = Corporal
Sgt. = Sergeant	Sgt. Maj. = Sergeant Major
Lt. = Lieutenant	Capt. = Captain
Maj. = Major	Lt. Col. = Lieutenant Colonel
Col. = Colonel	Sn. = Seaman
Musc. = Musician	H.S. = Hospital Steward
Qm. Sgt. = Quartermaster Sergeant	Comm. Sgt. = Commissary Sergeant
Asst. Surg. = assistant surgeon	Surg. = Surgeon
Mtd. = Mounted	V.R.C. = Veteran Reserve Corps
Inf. = Infantry	Cav. = Cavalry
Art. = Artillery	H.A. = Heavy Artillery
L.A. = Light Artillery	N/A = not applicable

An asterisk (*) behind the last name on the cemetery lists indicates that the veteran has a <u>civilian</u> stone. However, some names were added later while cross referencing and may or may not have government stones.

CIVIL WAR ARMY STRUCTURE

Comrades-in-battle – 4 men grouped together
Platoon – ½ of a company – 50 men
Company – 100 men
Regiment – 1,000 men (10 companies)
Brigade – 4 to 5,000 men (4 to 5 regiments)
Division – about 16,000 men (3 brigades)
Corps – about 48,000 men (3 to 4 divisions)
Army – 2 to 7 Corps

**Note: These numbers are by <u>regulation</u>. In actuality, attrition reduced the average Civil War regiment to about 400 men during the course of the war.

RANK STRUCTURE OF AN INFANTRY COMPANY
 (About 100 men)

Private – 82 men
Corporal – 8 men
Sergeant – 4 men
Commissary Sergeant – 1 man
Quartermaster Sergeant – 1 man
1st Sergeant (orderly sergeant) – 1 man
2nd Lieutenant – 1 man
1st Lieutenant – 1 man
Captain – 1 man

RANK STRUCTURE OF AN INFANTRY REGIMENT
(About 1,000 men on paper)

Ten companies to a regiment equaling 1,000 men. A staff was needed to command, supply, and serve the companies.
Colonel – 1 man – in command of the entire regiment.
Lieutenant Colonel – 1 man – second in command of the regiment.
Major – 1 man - third in command of the regiment.
Adjutant – 1 man with the rank of lieutenant – served as an aide to the three men above, performing reconnaissance, completing paperwork, etc.
Quartermaster – 1 man-with the rank of lieutenant - was responsible for keeping records of regimental supplies such as clothing and ammunition, and ordering more when needed.
Surgeon – 1 man – chief medical officer of the regiment.
Assistant Surgeon – 1 man – secondary medical officer of the regiment.
Chaplain – 1 man – responsible for caring for the spiritual side of the men in the regiment.
Sergeant Major – 1 man - head enlisted man in the regiment, acted as a liaison between the officers and enlisted men.
Quartermaster Sergeant – 1 man – assistant to the Quartermaster.
Commissary Sergeant – 1 man – responsible for making sure the regiment is supplied with rations.
Hospital Steward – 1 man – enlisted man that serves as an assistant to the Surgeon/Asst. Surgeon

Directory of Cemeteries

CEMETERY NAME	LOCATION	NUMBER OF VETERANS
Albert Cemetery	Mountain Top	10
Annunciation Cemetery	Shenandoah	48
Beach Grove Cemetery	Salem Township	5
Beach Haven Cemetery	Berwick	29
Beaver Meadows West Cem.	Beaver Meadows	7
Benton Cemetery	Benton	43
Bethany Cemetery	Barnesville	15
Bethel Hill Cemetery	Bethel Hill	17
Bible Church Cemetery	Sweet Valley	14
Black Creek Cemetery	Sugarloaf	2
Bloomingdale Cemetery	Bloomingdale	20
B'nai B'rith Cemetery	Hanover Township	1
Brainerd Cemetery	Seybertsville	1
Broadway Cemetery	Broadway	10
Bronson Road Cemetery	Hunlock Creek	2
Cambra Cemetery	Cambra	7
Carverton Methodist Cemetery	Carverton	28
Cathedral Cemetery	Scranton	208
Ceasdale Cemetery	Rt. 29, near Moon Lake park	18
Charles Baber Cemetery	Pottsville	319
Christ Cemetery	Fountain Springs	83
Church Hill Cemetery	Pittston	10
Church Street Cemetery	Catawissa	44
Citizen's Cemetery	Beaver Meadows	28
Clark's Green Cemetery	Clark Summit	69
Conyngham Episcopal Cem.	Conyngham	9
Conyngham Union Cem.	Conyngham	52
Creveling Cemetery	Almedia	73
Dodson Cemetery	Town Hill	26
Dunmore Cemetery	Dunmore	394
Duryea Cemetery	Duryea	14
Eatonville Baptist Cemetery	Eatonville	35
Ebenezer Cemetery	Orgville	5
Eckley Cemetery	Eckley	5
Edge Hill Cemetery	West Nanticoke	11
Emmanuel Cemetery	Dorrance	17
English Lutheran Cemetery	Seybertsville	3
English Zion Cemetery	Tamaqua	12
Evergreen Cemetery	Dallas	30
Evergreen Cemetery	Factoryville	93
Evergreen Cemetery	Jim Thorpe	57
Fairmount Springs Cemetery	Fairmount Township	31
Fairview Memorial Park	Elmhurst	25
Fern Knoll Cemetery	Center Hill Rd., Dallas	51
Forrest Hill Cemetery	Scranton	304
Forrest Home Cemetery	Taylor	17
Forty Fort Cemetery	Forty Fort	181
Freeland Cemetery	Freeland	63

Cemetery	Location	Count
Frenchtown Cemetery	Beaver Brook	14
Friedens Cemetery	Tamaqua	30
Garrison Cemetery	Berwick	6
German Catholic Cemetery	Pottsville	22
Grand Army Cemetery	Summit Hill	127
Hamlin Church Cemetery	Rt. 239, near Benton	14
Hamtown Cemetery	Pittston	11
Hanover Green Cemetery	Hanover Township	127
Hauck Family Cemetery	Quakake	1
Hollenback Cemetery	Wilkes-Barre	382
Hollisterville Cemetery	Hollisterville	21
Holy Trinity Cemetery	Hazleton	2
Hughestown Cemetery	Hughestown	22
Huntsville Cemetery	Huntsville	15
Immaculate Conception Cem.	Jim Thorpe	43
Jeansville Methodist Cemetery	Jeansville	49
Jenkins Cemetery	West Pittston	2
Jewish Cemetery	Pittston	1
Jonestown Methodist Cemetery	Jonestown	21
Laurel Cemetery	White Haven	128
Lehighton Cemetery	Lehighton	157
Lehman Center Cemetery	Lehman	29
Leteer Cemetery	Sweet Valley	2
Lime Ridge Cemetery	Lime Ridge	26
Maple Grove Cemetery	Sweet Valley	38
Maple Hill Cemetery	Hanover	73
Maplewood Cemetery	Carbondale	184
Marcy Cemetery	Duryea	120
Market Street Cemetery	Pittston	106
Martzville Cemetery	Berwick	8
Marvin Cemetery	Muhlenberg	34
Mauch Chunk Cemetery	Jim Thorpe	218
McKeansburg Cemetery	McKeansburg	13
Memorial Cemetery	Taylor	19
Methodist Cemetery	Blakeslee (corners)	3
Methodist Cemetery	Jeansville	48
Mifflinville Cemetery	Mifflinville	35
Millville Cemetery	Millville	38
Moscow Cemetery	Moscow	45
Mossville Cemetery	Mossville	26
Mount Carmel Cemetery	Dunmore	6
Mount Zion Cemetery	Kingston Twp.	14
Mount Zion Cemetery	Nescopeck	28
Mount Zion Cemetery	North Union Twp., Zion's Grove	12
Mount Zion Cemetery	Nuangola	20
Mount Zion Cemetery	Pittston	6
Mountain Grove Cemetery	Mountain Grove	22
Mountain View Cemetery	Exeter Township	6
Mountain View Cemetery	West Hazleton	39
Nanticoke Cemetery	Nanticoke	28
Nesquehoning Cemetery	Nesquehoning	26
New Columbus Cemetery	New Columbus	21
New Rosemont Cemetery	Espy	19
Noxen Cemetery	Noxen	34

Cemetery	Location	Count
Nuremburg Cemetery	Nuremburg	16
Oakdale Church Cemetery	Hunlock Creek	19
Oaklawn Cemetery	Hanover Township	72
Odd Fellow's Cemetery	Pottsville	140
Odd Fellow's Cemetery	Shenandoah	124
Odd Fellow's Cemetery	Tamaqua	323
Old Newport Township Cem.	Newport Township	16
Orangeville Cemetery	Orangeville	36
Orwigsburg Cemetery	Orwigsburg	68
Osterhout Cemetery	Osterhout	4
Parryville Cemetery	Parryville	17
Perrego Cemetery	Harveys Lake	4
Pine Center Methodist Cemetery	Pine Township	5
Pine Grove Cemetery	Berwick	164
Pine Grove Cemetery	Huntington Mills	30
Pine Hill Cemetery	Shickshinny	125
Pines Cemetery	Bear Creek	1
Pittston Ave. Cemetery	Scranton	32
Pittston City Cemetery	Pittston	98
Port Clinton Cemetery	Port Clinton	32
Presbyterian Cemetery	Pottsville	78
Presbyterian Cemetery	Summit Hill	45
Ransom Lutheran Cemetery	Ransom	5
Red Rock Cemetery	Red Rock	1
Rice Cemetery	Dallas	7
Ricketts Family Cemetery	Lake Ganoga	1
Roselawn Cemetery	Berwick	3
Rosemont Cemetery	Bloomsburg	222
Route 93 Cemetery	Conyngham	1
Sacred Heart Cemetery	Plains	17
Salem Methodist Cemetery	Unityville	29
Scott Cemetery	Huntington Mills	53
Shawnee Cemetery	Plymouth	113
Shoemaker Cemetery	Dalton	39
Sorber Cemetery	Reyburn	17
Sorbertown Cemetery	Sorbertown Hill	19
Spring Brook Cemetery	Spring Brook	39
St. Ann's Cemetery	Freeland	14
St. Gabriel's Cemetery	Hazleton	71
St. Ignatius Cemetery	Kingston	14
St. James Cemetery	Bendertown	15
St. James Cemetery	Nescopeck	9
St. James' Church Cem.	Hobbie	5
St. Jerome's Cemetery	Tamaqua	23
St. John's Cemetery	Brandonville	3
St. John's Cemetery	Drums	38
St. John's Cemetery	New Mahoning	22
St. John's Cemetery	Ringtown	18
St. John's Church Cem.	Brandonville	2
St. John's German Church	Sheppton	1
St. Joseph's Cemetery	Jim Thorpe	6
St. Joseph's Cemetery	Scranton	4
St. Mark's Cemetery	Lily Lake	4
St. Mary's Cemetery	Avoca	15

Cemetery	Location	Count
St. Mary's Cemetery	Beaver Meadows	1
St. Mary's Cemetery	Hanover Township	100
St. Mary's Cemetery	Scranton	5
St. Mary's Church Cemetery	Pittston	1
St. Matthew's Church Cem.	Weatherly	4
St. Nicholas' Cemetery	Shavertown	2
St. Nicholas' Cemetery	Weatherly	2
St. Nicholas' Cemetery	Wilkes-Barre	23
St. Patrick's Cemetery	McAdoo	12
St. Patrick's Cemetery	White Haven	4
St. Paul's Cemetery	Drums	21
St. Peter's Cemetery	Andreas	6
St. Peter's Cemetery	Barnesville	14
St. Peter's Cemetery	Briar Creek Twp., off Rt. 11 S. of Berwick	24
St. Peter's Church Cem.	Hobbie	4
St. Rose's Cemetery	Carbondale	54
St. Vincent's Cemetery	Larksville	37
Stillwater Cemetery	Benton	5
Sugar Notch Cemetery	Sugar Notch	7
Summer Hill Cemetery	Summer Hill	11
Sweet Valley Cemetery	Sweet Valley	9
Thornhurst Cemetery	Thornhurst	5
Tunkhannock Cemetery	Tunkhannock	106
Union Cemetery	Weatherly	125
Union Hill Cemetery	Weissport	29
Upper Lehigh Cemetery	Upper Lehigh	4
Vine Street Cemetery	Hazleton	297
Waller Cemetery	Benton	23
Washburn Street Cemetery	Scranton	222
Weissport Cemetery	Weissport	36
West Pittston Cemetery	West Pittston	183
White Church Cemetery	Quakake	23
White Church Cemetery	Ringtown	32
White Church Cemetery	Trucksville	60
Wilkes-Barre City Cemetery	Wilkes-Barre	196
Willing Street Cemetery	Tamaqua	11
Woodlawn Cemetery	Dallas	34
Wyoming Cemetery	Wyoming	88
Zion Stone Church Cemetery	Snyders	38
	TOTAL	**9,226**

Biographies in this Book

pg. 16	Lieutenant Alonzo Bennett – Co. K, 81st Pennsylvania Volunteer Infantry
pg. 20	Corporal Charles W. Ridgway – Co. E, 203rd P.V.I.
pg. 24	Private Ezra Ripple – Co. K, 52nd P.V.I.
pg. 28	Lieutenant Franklin Brockway – Battery F, 1st PA Light Artillery (43rd Regiment of the line)
pg. 32	Private George Geary – Co. I, 81st P.V.I.
pg. 36	Colonel Henry M. Hoyt – Staff, 52nd P.V.I.
pg. 40	Lieutenant Colonel Eugene B. Beaumont - Staff, 4th U.S. Cavalry
pg. 44	Sergeant James M. Rutter – Co. C, 143rd P.V.I.
pg. 48	Captain James Post – Co. F, 149th P.V.I.
pg. 52	Major Lansford F. Chapman – Staff, 28th P.V.I.
pg. 56	Private Samuel M. Callendar - Co. L, 2nd Pennsylvania Heavy Artillery (112th Regiment of the line)
pg. 60	Private Stephen Gregory – Co. B, 58th P.V.I.
pg. 64	Lieutenant Colonel Thomas Harkness – Staff, 81st P.V.I.
pg. 68	Lieutenant William F. Bloss – Co. H, 76th P.V.I.
pg. 72	Private Wilson Beers – Co. K, 81st P.V.I.
pg. 76	Lieutenant Colonel Eli T. Conner – Staff, 81st P.V.I.
pg. 80	Lieutenant Patrick DeLacy – Co. A, 143rd P.V.I.
pg. 85	Frederick L. Hitchcock – Major, 132nd P.V.I., and Colonel, 25th U.S. Colored Regiment
pg. 90	Corporal Benjamin Sharpless – Co. A, 6th PA Reserves (35th Regiment of the line)
pg. 93	Private Charles C. Betterly – Co. C, 143rd P.V.I.
pg. 96	Corporal Chester Furman – Co. A, 6th PA Reserves (35th Regiment of the line)
pg. 99	Colonel Edmund L. Dana – Staff, 143rd P.V.I.
pg. 102	Private Eli E. Corwin – Co. B, 17th PA Cavalry (162nd Regiment of the line)
pg. 104	Corporal George Schlager – Co. A, 4th PA Cavalry (64th Regiment of the line)
pg. 108	Private George W. Engle – Co. A, 143rd P.V.I.
pg. 111	Private Henry Krigbaum – Co. I, 132nd P.V.I.
pg. 114	Sergeant Hiram Pursell – Co. G, 104th P.V.I.
pg. 117	Captain Isaac Severn – Co. C, 96th P.V.I.
pg. 120	Private Andrew Lape – Co. D, 9th PA Cavalry (92nd Regiment of the line)
pg. 122	Corporal James J. Maycock – Co. I, 132nd P.V.I.
pg. 125	Corporal John S. Short – Co. K, 132nd P.V.I.
pg. 128	Corporal Moses Morris – Co. D, 54th Massachusetts Infantry
pg. 132	Captain Robert B. Ricketts – Battery F, 1st PA Light Artillery (43rd Regiment of the line)
pg. 135	Captain Sylvester Rhodes – Co. D, 61st P.V.I.
pg. 138	Colonel Wellington Ent – Staff, 6th PA Reserves
pg. 141	The Tubbs Brothers – Elias, Joseph, Josiah, and Daniel, of the 143rd, 7th Reserves, 143rd, and 199th regiments respectively.
pg. 148	Corporal David M. Jones – Co. I, 199th P.V.I.
pg. 151	Merritt S. Harding – Corporal, Co. B, 12th PA Reserves (41st Regiment of the line) and Lieutenant, Co. C, 127th U.S. Colored Regiment

RYAN LINDBUCHLER

ALONZO EDWARD BENNETT
June 16, 1833 – May 28, 1867

Alonzo Bennett was born in Carbon County, Pennsylvania. Little is known about his early childhood except that it was most likely spent in Carbon and Luzerne Counties. When he was a young man of working age, he was employed as a painter. Later, he learned the skills of an engineer.

By the age of twenty-five, Bennett was working as an engineer and was living in the mining town of Eckley, Luzerne County. In 1859, he met and married a local woman, Isabella Bayne, at a small Presbyterian church in Eckley. When war erupted in 1861, Bennett was eager to serve his country, as were many other Eckley men.

A neighbor, Charles E. Foster, was raising a company of infantry to be attached to a three-year regiment. Bennett enlisted in Company K of the 81st Pennsylvania Volunteer Infantry Regiment as first Sergeant on October 27, 1861. Company K was made up mostly of Eckley residents, and probably friends of Bennett. According to company records, he was listed as being twenty-eight years of age, 5' 11 ½" in height, having sandy colored hair, brown eyes, and a fair complexion.

The regiment was trained outside Washington and was attached to the 1st Brigade, 1st Division, II Corps, where it would remain for the entire war. It was engaged for the first time at Fair Oaks in May of 1862 where its colonel, James Miller, was killed. Bennett and the rest of the regiment next fought at Yorktown, Savage Station, White Oak Swamp, Glendale, Charles City Crossroads, and Malvern Hill, taking heavy casualties. Bennett was fortunate, escaping all battles unhurt. However, regimental leadership was devastated. Colonel Charles Johnson was wounded at Charles City Crossroads and Lieutenant Colonel Eli T. Conner was killed at Malvern Hill.

By August, 1862, Bennett found himself second in command of Company K. When Lieutenant Cyrus Straw was wounded in the assault on the sunken road at the Battle of Antietam, company command passed to Bennett, and he led the company through death and carnage for the remainder of the day. The next December, he and his company took part in the fruitless assaults on Marye's Heights at the Battle of Fredericksburg. The company, as well as the regiment, was devastated as a result. Bennett again escaped without injury but perhaps wondered what the next year might bring.

In the spring of 1863, the army found itself commanded by General Joseph Hooker, who eagerly looked for his chance to turn the course of the war in favor of the North with a decisive victory over Confederate General Robert E. Lee. His chance came in May of 1863 at the Battle of Chancellorsville. The battle was a disaster for Hooker and the Union cause. The II Corps and the regiment were lightly engaged during the first two days of this battle (May 1, 2), but was used as a rear guard for retreating Federal troops of the V Corps on May 3, 1863. The 81st regiment helped repel a substantial Confederate offensive and sustained considerable loss. First Sgt. Alonzo Bennett was one of these casualties. Regimental Surgeon John Houston wrote the following in camp near Petersburg, Virginia, in August of 1864:

> This is to certify that amputation was necessary in the case of Lieutenant A.E. Bennett, Co. K, 81st PA Vols. His (left) arm having been nearly carried away by solid shot at the battle of Chancellorsville.

Following his wounding, Bennett was commissioned a First Lieutenant on July 13, 1863. He returned home to Eckley briefly to recover and then joined the Veteran Reserve Corps. The V.R.C., or "Invalid Corps," was a portion of the Federal army that served behind the front lines in various capacities such as prison guards, garrison troops surrounding Washington, D.C., assistants at hospitals, and clerks. The purpose of the Veteran Reserve Corps was to free up able-bodied men to serve at the front. Bennett served as First Lieutenant of the 4th Regiment at Rock Island and Springfield, Illinois until July of 1866 when the regiment was mustered out of service. During his service in the V.R.C., he learned of the death of his brother, Eugene, in July of 1864. He was serving as a private in Company C of the 147th Pennsylvania Volunteer Infantry and was mortally wounded at the Battle of Pine Knob, later dying in a hospital at Chattanooga, Tennessee.

Alonzo and Isabella Bennett had two children during the course of their marriage: Eugene B. in 1865 and Rebecca in 1867. Bennett returned from Illinois to join his family in very poor health. According to his physician, he was in "very delicate health" and was suffering from dropsy and pneumonia as a result of his service in the military. However, he provided an income for his young family by serving as a timekeeper for the Lehigh Valley Railroad in the two years following his discharge. His health would continue to deteriorate, resulting in his death at Delano on May 28, 1867, with his wife and doctor at his side. He died from the wound he sustained four years previous.

Isabella received a pension of $17 per month. She returned to Eckley and was again devastated in 1883, when her son Eugene was declared insane and committed to a mental hospital at Danville, Pennsylvania. He would live out the remainder of his life in mental hospitals until his death in 1923. Her last child, Rebecca, died at the age of eight, in 1875, leaving Isabella alone until her death in 1923.

Bennett was laid to rest at the Mauch Chunk Cemetery and was later joined by his wife upon her death. One may visit their resting-place there today. Many of Bennett's comrades from the 81st Pennsylvania Infantry rest in the same cemetery, including Lieutenant Colonel Eli T. Conner who was killed at Malvern Hill, Lieutenant Colonel Amos Stroh who commanded the regiment for some time, and Captain Charles E. Foster who originally recruited Alonzo into Company K at Eckley.

Gone But Not Forgotten | *Civil War Veterans of Northeastern Pennsylvania*

Lieutenant Alonzo Bennett, Co. K, 81st Pennsylvania Volunteer Infantry
Credit: U.S. Army Military History Institute Collection

ALONZO BENNETT, MAUCH CHUNK CEMETERY, JIM THORPE
CREDIT: KRISTEN LINDBUCHLER PHOTO

CHARLES W. RIDGWAY
June 17, 1845 – October 9, 1923

In Fishkill, New York, a son was born to Mr. and Mrs. Allanse Ridgway. His name was Charles. The couple would have eleven children in all, and hoped their children might grow up to become loyal, responsible Americans. On the family farm, the boy grew to become a man and learned what responsibility and hard work were all about. The large family moved to Luzerne County when Ridgway was a teenager and settled on a larger, more profitable farm.

When war came in 1861, Ridgway was only sixteen years old, and perhaps longed to take part in the adventures of soldiering. The monotony of farm life in a crowded house with ten brothers and sisters may have also influenced his will to become a soldier. However, Army regulations required men to be at least eighteen years of age to be eligible to serve in the military. When news of exciting and heroic battles at such places as Antietam and Gettysburg reached his ears throughout the years 1862 and 1863, his will to serve was most certainly strengthened. His chance came in September of 1864.

The nineteen-year-old farm boy enlisted at Scranton in Company E of the 203rd Pennsylvania Volunteer Infantry Regiment. Company rolls list him as being 5'6-1/2" tall, having blue eyes, brown hair, and a dark (probably sun tanned) complexion. The 203rd was called "Birney's Sharpshooters" because it was the original intention of General David B. Birney to train the regiment as sharpshooters for a division in the X Corps. Birney died, however, and the 203rd served as a typical infantry regiment. Ridgway, like the others in his company, enlisted for a period of one year and received a bounty of $100.

Ridgway said goodbye to his parents, brothers and sisters, and left Scranton with the regiment, bound for the Army of the James. The 203rd regiment was attached to the X Corps as it was engaged in the siege of Petersburg, Virginia. It arrived at the front on September 27 and was immediately detached to Deep Bottom to escort prisoners to the rear and perform picket duty. Following this duty, it was sent back to the front where it took part in another skirmish at Darbytown Road, where it lost seven men. Ridgway took part in the actions and remained unscathed.

The 203rd regiment was reassigned to the XXIV Corps and immediately sent to Fort Monroe, Virginia, where it prepared to assault Fort Fisher, on the North Carolina coast. Fort Fisher was an important objective for the Union army because it guarded the important port of Wilmington. Most of the other Confederate ports had been closed by Union forces, but Wilmington remained

as a source of supply for the Confederate cause. On January 2, 1865, the regiment was part of the initial assaulting force that was responsible for breaching the walls of the fort and capturing its parapets and guns. The 203rd charged forward, led by its colonel, and took heavy losses in the hail of bullets and grapeshots that were fired at them. Colonel Moore took the colors and inspired the men to follow him in the assault on the traverses. He fell, mortally wounded, along with almost half (about two-hundred men) of the regiment. Soon, the defenders were forced to surrender and the fort fell to the Union men.

One of those men wounded was a farmboy from Luzerne County named Charles Ridgway. During the assault, he had been engaged with the enemy in hand to hand fighting, when he was struck in the right shoulder and taken out of the fight. The wound was not serious and he recovered quickly enough to rejoin the regiment by the end of the month. He took part in the capture of Wilmington, North Carolina and was promoted to corporal on March 1. The regiment occupied Raleigh, North Carolina, and remained there until it was mustered out of service on June 22, 1865.

Ridgway returned home and took residence at Factoryville, Pennsylvania, where he met a woman named Amelia F. Reynolds. A courtship ensued and the couple was married at Waverly, Pennsylvania, on March 10, 1866. Together, they had four children: Clark, 1867; Ruth, 1870 (died in infancy); Allen, 1873; and Arthur, 1876 (died in infancy).

Ridgway was employed as a brakeman at the DL&W Railroad near Scranton. In 1891, he suffered an injury while on the job when his right hand was crushed while attempting to couple two cars. In 1880, the family moved to Penn Avenue in Scranton where they spent the remainder of their lives together. Ridgway received a pension from the government in the amount of $19 in 1915 because of his shoulder injury, rheumatism, and kidney disease. At the time of his death in 1923, he was an active member in the Scranton G.A.R. Upon his death, he was buried in the Dunmore Cemetery where one can visit his resting-place today.

Gone But Not Forgotten | *Civil War Veterans of Northeastern Pennsylvania*

CORPORAL CHARLES W. RIDGWAY, CO. E, 203RD PENNSYLVANIA VOLUNTEER INFANTRY
CREDIT: G.A.R. POST 139 COLLECTION

Ryan Lindbuchler

Charles Ridgway, about 1883
Credit: G.A.R. Post 139 Collection

EZRA HOYT RIPPLE
February 14, 1842 – November 19, 1909

Ezra Ripple was born of German and English descent to Silas and Elizabeth Ripple on a winter's day in Mauch Chunk, Pennsylvania. He attended common schools at Buck Mountain and then Wyoming Seminary in Kingston, Pennsylvania. Upon his graduation in 1858, he worked at his father's hotel in Scranton, but after his father's death in 1861, pursued the trade of druggist. He perhaps felt that the war might pass him by if he did not volunteer soon.

His chance to serve came in the summer of 1863 when Confederate General Robert E. Lee's Army of Northern Virginia attempted to invade the Northern States during the Gettysburg Campaign. The 13th Pennsylvania Militia was being formed as emergency troops, and Ripple helped raise Company H. He served as a sergeant with the 13th Militia for the short time that it was in existence, and that taste of army life motivated him to join Company K of the famed "Luzerne Regiment," or 52nd Pennsylvania Volunteer Infantry, in March of 1864.

The 52nd Regiment, raised in 1861, had served the Union for three years in the Deep South, attempting to capture various Confederate coastal fortifications. Made up of men from northeastern Pennsylvania, it was led by Colonel Henry M. Hoyt, the future governor of Pennsylvania and the subject of another biography in this book. When Ripple joined his regiment in the spring of 1864, it was made up largely of new recruits, mixed with many veterans of the past three years. In July, 1864, the 52nd was ordered to attack Fort Johnson, guarding Charleston, South Carolina. Ripple and the regiment undertook a night assault and were able to breach the walls of the fortress, but were forced to surrender when reinforcements did not arrive to bolster the attack. Ripple, as well as his colonel, became a prisoner of war.

Ripple and the other men were taken to Charleston and then to the infamous Andersonville prison in Georgia. There he suffered a fate that he could not have imagined when he enlisted. Andersonville was perhaps the worst prison camp that a northern prisoner of war might have had the misfortune of being sent. Shelter, food, and human decency were scarce commodities at this hell on earth. After the war, Ripple published his memoirs, entitled <u>Dancing Along the Deadline</u>, in which he tells of the suffering he and his comrades endured while imprisoned there. He was held there for about seventy-five days and then transferred to Florence, South Carolina, in October of 1864.

At Florence, Ripple decided to make an escape. He managed to get out of the compound, but an alarm was sounded and guards released bloodhounds into the surrounding swamps. Ripple, although weakened by malnutrition, was able to outrun the dogs for about four miles, but collapsing from exhaustion, he was viciously attacked by the bloodhounds and suffered several bites. Taken back to the prison camp, he came down with a fever and barely escaped death.

In March of 1865, Ripple had recovered from his wounds and was paroled. He was honorably discharged on June 30, 1865, at Annapolis, Maryland. Returning to Scranton, he enrolled in a business college at Poughkeepsie, New York. After graduation, he served as an administrator in the coal industry by 1872. In 1874, Ripple met and married Miss Sarah Hackett, the daughter of a Carbon County mine foreman. They would become the parents of four children: Hannah, Jessie, Susan, and Ezra H. Jr. In 1877, Ripple was elected captain of Company D of the Scranton City Guard, and then major of the 13th Regiment, Pennsylvania National Guard. Named colonel by 1888, he commanded the regiment until 1898.

He was elected the first treasurer of Lackawanna County when it was formed in 1878, and was elected mayor of Scranton in 1886. He served in this capacity until 1890, and during his term electricity was installed for lighting, roads were paved with asphalt, and an electric car system was constructed. In 1897, he was appointed postmaster of Scranton by President William McKinley. He would hold this post until his death in 1909.

Ripple belonged to several fraternal organizations through the remainder of his life, including Post 139, Grand Army of the Republic; Scranton Masonic lodge; and the Episcopal Church of Scranton. Ripple, the great public servant and soldier, passed away while performing his duties as postmaster in November of 1909 and was interred at the Dunmore Cemetery, where one may visit his resting place today. Ezra Ripple was considered a great man of his time and was much admired by the people of Scranton for generations. He will never be forgotten.

Gone But Not Forgotten | *Civil War Veterans of Northeastern Pennsylvania*

Private Ezra H. Ripple, Co. K, 52nd Pennsylvania Volunteer Infantry
Credit: G.A.R. Post 139 Collection

Ezra H. Ripple, Dunmore Cemetery Credit: Ryan Lindbuchler Photo

Franklin P. Brockway
February 8, 1845 – September 12, 1940

In the lush farmlands surrounding Berwick, Pennsylvania, two sons were born to Mr. and Mrs. Beckwith Brockway. Little did their parents suspect that their sons Charles and Franklin would grow up to fight in the bloodiest American conflict ever to take place. Beckwith taught his sons the skills of the farmer and shoemaker, and the boys were expected to become men who would be hardworking, upright citizens like their father. Fate would determine that they would become soldiers first.

When the war broke out in 1861, Charles was twenty-one and his younger brother Franklin was sixteen. Ten days after the opening shots of the Civil War were fired at Fort Sumter, South Carolina, Charles rushed off to join the "Iron Guards" at Bloomsburg. The company would later be known as Company A of the 6th Pennsylvania Reserves. Charles was enlisted as a sergeant and served in the regiment until the fall of 1861, when he was transferred to Battery F of the 1st Pennsylvania Light Artillery.

In January, 1862, officers of the battery were recruiting in Berwick. Franklin, wanting to serve in the army with his older brother, was able to join the battery as a private. Army regulations required that recruits be at least eighteen in order to serve, but many boys lied about their age in order to enlist. It is not known how Franklin was able to enlist, but it is most likely that his older brother intervened on his behalf. Military records show that Franklin Brockway was 5'5" in height, had blue eyes, light hair, and a light complexion. It must have been difficult for his parents to let their young sons go off to fight in a war that was being conducted hundreds of miles away, resulting in the deaths of thousands of young boys like the Brockways.

Captain Ezra W. Matthews, who would later be promoted to higher ranks, commanded the battery. The brothers traveled south and joined the battery at Hagerstown, Maryland. Charles was promoted to second lieutenant and given command of a detachment (not a full battery) of guns. It is not known whether Franklin served in his brother's detachment, but it seems most likely. During the Civil War, light artillery regiments were broken up into batteries and distributed among infantry and cavalry divisions, to support those troops in the field. Battery F was sent from Hagerstown to take part in operations in the Shenandoah Valley of Virginia, where it fought several skirmishes with the enemy under the command of Confederate General Stonewall Jackson. The battery next took part in the Battle of Second Bull Run and lost several men in the action. In the actions immediately following this engagement the battery lost twenty-

eight men. Lieutenant Charles Brockway was captured during this period, along with four other men. Franklin eluded capture, but was concerned about his older brother, who was imprisoned at the Confederate capital in Richmond.

The battery participated in the action at Antietam with the I Corps on September 17, 1862, near the now famous "Cornfield" where it was responsible for inflicting many casualties on attacking Confederate Infantry. The battery lost nineteen men and just about all their horses, with Captain Matthews' horse being shot out from under him during the battle. Brockway survived the action without a scratch. Soon after the battle, Matthews left on sick leave, never to return to battery command, and Lieutenant Robert B. Ricketts assumed command for the remainder of the war.

After participating in the battle of Fredericksburg in December, the battery went into winter quarters at Belle Plain in order to recover from the hard fighting of 1862. To Franklin's relief, his brother Charles was exchanged and returned to the battery that winter. The refitted battery took part in the Battle of Chancellorsville in May of 1863, being exposed to sniper and infantry fire. At Gettysburg, the battery withstood an infantry charge and fought hand to hand in order to hold its position and guns. For more detail on the actions at Gettysburg, refer to the biography of Captain Robert B. Ricketts. After Gettysburg, the battery was assigned to the II Corps and fought at Mine Run and Bristoe Station, going into winter quarters by December of 1863.

In May of 1864 at the Battle of the Wilderness, the battery fought bravely using canister, which inflicted many casualties. The guns were perilously close to being captured in the action, but infantry was called in and the battery withdrew, having spent its ammunition. Attached to the XVIII Corps, the battery then took part in the Battle of Cold Harbor and the siege of Petersburg. While taking part in the siege, Franklin Brockway was promoted to second lieutenant on December 21. Charles was discharged in October, being brevetted to the rank of captain in March of the following year. When Petersburg fell in April of 1865, the battery was sent to City Point, Virginia, and then to Washington, where it turned over its horses and guns. Franklin was mustered out of service on June 9, 1865, and returned to Berwick.

Soon after the war, Franklin moved to Wilkes-Barre to work as a brickmaker. While living there, he met and married a local woman named Cora. The couple was married in June of 1868 in Wilkes-Barre. The next year, a son Harvey was born to the couple. They would have four more children through the course of their lives together: Lizzie in 1871; Ella in 1873; Mary in 1874; and Roland in 1877.

In 1889, Brockway moved back to Berwick to once again become a farmer. However, farming did not suit Brockway, and he soon moved to Beach Haven, just outside Berwick in 1894, to serve as president of the First National Bank of Berwick. In November of 1912, Cora died of unknown causes, leaving the sixty-seven year old veteran on his own. Brockway would again find love and married Louisa Armsby on February 12, 1915, at Fort Myers, Florida. In 1912 Brockway had received a pension in the amount of $19 per month on the grounds of rheumatism and heart disease. In 1938, the amount was increased to $75 per month.

In July of 1940, at the age of ninety-five, Franklin P. Brockway was one of the oldest remaining Civil War veterans from northeastern Pennsylvania. At his home on a hot July day, Brockway tripped and fell, breaking his hip. He was immediately taken to Berwick by his son Roland for medical care. He never recovered and died there two months later. The old veteran was buried in the Beach Haven Cemetery among twenty-eight other veterans of the conflict that tore our nation apart. The burial place of Charles Brockway is not known to the author.

Gone But Not Forgotten | *Civil War Veterans of Northeastern Pennsylvania*

Lieutenant Franklin P. Brockway, Battery F, 1st Pennsylvania Light Artillery
Credit: U.S. Army Military History Institute Collection

Ryan Lindbuchler

Captain Charles Brockway, Battery F, 1st Pennsylvania Light Artillery
Credit: Gerry Leister Collection

GEORGE GEARY
September 7, 1847 – March 27, 1924

In 1847, George Geary was born the third child to the Gearys, a Methodist family that lived in Pittston. When compared to today's society, childhood in the Victorian period was relatively short. At the age of ten, Geary was sent to live with his uncle, William Jacobs, near West Pittston to learn the trade of a machinist. When war broke out in 1861, he was fourteen and still an apprentice at his uncle's business. By all indications, he wanted very much to join the army, but of course was too young to do so. In 1862, Geary moved to the home of Louis Davenport, at Hazleton, Pennsylvania, to practice his newly acquired skills as a machinist.

Life in Hazleton was not exciting enough for Geary, who longed to be a soldier on far off battlefields, fighting epic battles that would change the course of history. In youth, war sometimes seems glorious, but in reality is death, destruction, and carnage on a grand scale. In June of 1863, Geary deceved army recruiters and joined Captain Henry Brown's Independent Company of Cavalry, under the false statement that he was eighteen. The regiment was known as the Luzerne Rangers Volunteers of Pennsylvania, and was a state militia organization. This militia company was formed during Confederate General Robert E. Lee's invasion of Pennsylvania, as an emergency regiment to resist this invasion. The invasion was stopped with a Union victory at Gettysburg in July, and the regiment was disbanded on August 1, 1863, never having heard a shot fired in anger.

Following his sixteenth birthday, Geary was even more determined to see the face of combat. In February of 1864, recruiting officers from the 81st Pennsylvania Volunteer Infantry Regiment were in Mauch Chunk (modern day Jim Thorpe) in Carbon County to enlist men to serve in Company I of that regiment. The men of the original company had been recruited from Carbon County in 1861, and recruits were needed to replenish the ranks left empty by casualties sustained at battles such as Fair Oaks, Charles City Crossroads, Antietam, Fredericksburg, Chancellorsville and Gettysburg. Geary again deceved officers and eagerly took the oath to serve the Union. Government records list him as being 5'6" tall, having gray eyes, a light complexion and light hair.

By March, Geary had joined the regiment near Brandy Station, Virginia. The men of the 81st regiment were now considered "veteran volunteers" for their hard service through the first three years of the war. The few veterans that remained had to teach the new recruits, like Geary, how to become good soldiers. The task was accomplished by May, and the regiment was ready to take

the field with the II Corps in the spring campaign. Geary "saw the elephant" (was in a battle) for the first time at the Battle of the Wilderness. The 81st regiment took considerable losses in the action that was fought in a dense forest in northern Virginia. On May 12, the II Corps, along with the 81st regiment, assaulted enemy earthworks at Spotsylvania Court House and captured two defensive lines, hundreds of prisoners, several cannons, and many enemy flags. During this battle a private in Company H, Thomas Robinson, charged out in front of the regiment and seized a Confederate flag from the enemy colorbearer. Geary watched as Robinson grasped the staff and demoralized the enemy. For that action, Robinson was awarded the Congressional Medal of Honor.

On June 3, Geary took part in the disastrous Federal assault at Cold Harbor and again came out of the fight unscathed. The regiment next served in the siege of Petersburg, taking part in several battles around it, such as Strawberry Plains, Ream's Station, and Deep Bottom. Each time the regiment distinguished itself and never lost its colors.

By March of 1865, the Confederates holding Petersburg were forced to abandon the city, and the Union army set out on a chase of Lee's retreating columns. From the close of the month until the surrender of Lee at Appomattox on April 9, the 81st regiment was worn down by constant marching and by meeting the enemy several times in severe skirmishes. During one of the skirmishes on March 31, 1865, Private George Geary was shot in the left arm just above the elbow and was almost deafened by Confederate artillery fire that exploded around him in the fight. His limp body was immediately taken to the II Corps hospital for treatment. The minie ball was removed and he was sent to City Point, Virginia, and then to the hospital steamer "Cosmopolitan," where he was transported to a permanent hospital at Washington. There, he recovered from his arm wound and was discharged from the army on June 2, 1865.

The seventeen-year-old returned to Mauch Chunk a veteran of many battles, with total deafness in his left ear and severe deafness in the other. He returned to the life of a machinist and lived in Mauch Chunk until 1872. That year, Geary moved to Scranton, Pennsylvania and met a Kingston woman by the name of Lillian Stevens. A courtship ensued, and the couple was married in Kingston on March 28, 1877. For the remainder of his life, Geary received an army pension for his deafness, as well as for the pains he suffered in his left arm. In 1899 he was receiving a pension of $22 per month. This was increased every few years until his death in 1924. Upon his death, he was interred in the Forrest Hill Cemetery in Scranton, where his grave is marked by a simple headstone. In life, Geary was typical of his generation. He became a man through his experiences in a savage, bloody civil war.

Gone But Not Forgotten | *Civil War Veterans of Northeastern Pennsylvania*

PRIVATE GEORGE GEARY, CO. I, 81ST PENNSYLVANIA VOLUNTEER INFANTRY
CREDIT: G.A.R. POST 139 COLLECTION

Ryan Lindbuchler

George Geary, about 1890
Credit: G.A.R. Post 139 Collection

Henry Martyn Hoyt
June 8, 1830 – December 1, 1892

Henry M. Hoyt wore many hats throughout his lifetime. He served as schoolteacher, lawyer, soldier, judge and statesman. Through his years of public service and devotion to country, he exemplified a true patriot.

Born in Kingston Township at the family farm, Hoyt learned what hard work and dedication could accomplish. At the age of eighteen, in 1848, he graduated from Williams College and began teaching at Wyoming Seminary in Kingston, Pennsylvania. From there he began studying law and was admitted to the bar in 1853.

When war came in 1861, Hoyt saw his patriotic duty and left his law practice in the spring of that year to help recruit the 52nd Pennsylvania Volunteer Infantry Regiment, nicknamed the "Luzerne Regiment," because many of the men that made up the regiment were volunteer citizens from Luzerne County. Upon completion of recruitment, Hoyt was commissioned lieutenant colonel of the regiment.

He served as second in command of the regiment through the thickest of the fighting during McClellan's Peninsula Campaign at such battles as Yorktown, Fair Oaks, and Seven Pines. The regiment was transferred south with the rest of the Corps to serve as part of the Union force assigned to capture southern coastal fortifications along the eastern seaboard.

By January of 1864, Hoyt had been promoted to the rank of colonel and was charged with commanding the regiment. By July of 1864, the regiment, along with others, was given the task of capturing forts around Charleston, South Carolina. Hoyt, along with 135 men of the 52nd landed on the beach surrounding Confederate Fort Johnson with the task of leading an assault on the fort. The men of the 52nd were able to breach the walls of the fort and gain entry, but no support was sent and the men, including Hoyt, were forced to surrender to superior numbers. The enlisted men of the 52nd were sent to prisons at Columbia, South Carolina and Andersonville, Georgia. One of these enlisted men, Private Ezra Ripple of Company K, is the subject of another short biography contained in this book. Henry, like the other officers, was sent to Macon, Georgia, and then to Charleston, South Carolina for imprisonment. During the Civil War, officers were imprisoned at separate facilities from enlisted men.

Hoyt suffered great hardships during his imprisonment, but was paroled by November of 1864 and mustered out of service on November 5. Four months later, Hoyt would learn that he had been given the rank of brevet brigadier general by the army for his meritorious conduct in the field.

After the war, Hoyt returned to his law practice in Wilkes-Barre, and was appointed judge of Luzerne County courts in 1867. He served as collector of revenue in his district from 1869 to 1873, and ran for the office of governor of Pennsylvania in 1878. He won the election and was inaugurated in January of 1879. As governor, Hoyt introduced a reform of the state penal system. He introduced a reformatory system for first offenders that created the Industrial Reformatory at Huntingdon, which separated first offenders from hardened criminals. This gesture of mercy for first time offenders was typical of Hoyt's actions as a leader. Also under his administration, Hoyt attempted to resolve pay disputes between the state government and employees. He was criticized by his political opponents for taking a strong position, but was considered a fair and reasonable leader of the Commonwealth.

Shortly after his service as governor, Hoyt retired to a quiet life in Wilkes-Barre, enjoying the study of philosophy, history, and politics. However, by 1890, an illness had weakened Hoyt. This illness eventually resulted in his death at his home in Wilkes-Barre in December of 1892. His death was mourned across the Commonwealth and flags flew at half-mast for days.

His remains were interred at the Forty Fort Cemetery shortly thereafter where they survived the great Agnes flood of 1972 which destroyed the final resting place of hundreds of the deceased interred there. Today, one can visit his grave and ponder the greatness of the man and his deeds.

Gone But Not Forgotten | *Civil War Veterans of Northeastern Pennsylvania*

COLONEL HENRY M. HOYT, STAFF, 52ND PENNSYLVANIA VOLUNTEER INFANTRY
CREDIT: ROGER D. HUNT COLLECTION

Henry M. Hoyt, Forty Fort Cemetery
Credit: Kristen Lindbuchler Photo

EUGENE BEAUHARNAIS BEAUMONT
August 2, 1837 – July 17, 1916

On May 10, 1865, Confederate President Jefferson Davis was captured by a Michigan cavalry regiment near Irwinsville, Georgia. Since the fall of the Confederate capital at Richmond, Virginia, in March, the Confederate government was forced into exile. Davis fled to Georgia in hopes of linking up with a small Confederate force, but Federal troops caught up with him, and he was arrested. When Davis was returned as a prisoner to headquarters at Macon, Georgia, he was received by Colonel Eugene B. Beaumont, who was personally responsible for guarding Davis until he was sent north to be imprisoned at Fort Monroe, Virginia, until his trial (which actually never occurred).

The experiences that would lead this young man to performing this prestigious duty began with his birth at Wilkes-Barre in 1837. He was the son of a local lawyer, Andrew Beaumont, and was well educated as a boy. He attended the U.S. military academy at West Point in the late 1850s, graduating in May of 1861. The young officer would quickly put his training to work fighting for the Union cause. He was immediately commissioned a second lieutenant with the 1st U.S. Cavalry and sent south to Washington to drill volunteers in the art of the cavalryman. By June of 1861, he was appointed to the staff of General Ambrose Burnside. He performed admirably during the Battle of First Bull Run in July of 1861, and was commended by Burnside for his performance.

Beaumont returned home to Wilkes-Barre in September to marry Miss Margaret Rutter, daughter of Nathaniel Rutter and sister of James M. Rutter (Medal of Honor winner of the 143rd PA Infantry). Together the couple would have four children: Natalie, Hortense, Eugene, and Andre.

The fall of 1861 brought a new assignment to Beaumont. He was assigned to act as aide-de-camp to General John Sedgwick. He served in this capacity admirably during several battles of the Peninsula Campaign, but was forced to leave the field in 1862, afflicted with a case of typhoid fever. Upon his return to the army, he was assigned to serve as aide-de-camp to General Henry Halleck, the general-in-chief of Union armies. He served in this capacity during the remainder of 1862 and through May of 1863. Duty as aide-de-camp to General Halleck was consumed with much deskwork and little action.

Beaumont, perhaps bored with his mundane duties, requested a transfer to the Army of the Potomac. His request was granted, and he was once again assigned to act as captain and aide-de-camp to Major General John Sedgwick, then commanding the VI Corps. The corps would take part in the Gettysburg campaign and be engaged several times in the spring campaign of

1864. At the Battle of the Wilderness in May of 1864, Beaumont was at the side of General Sedgwick when he was killed by a sharpshooter. He remained as aide-de-camp to the new corps commander through the battles of Spotsylvania Court House and Cold Harbor.

In June of 1864, General Ulysses S. Grant ordered Beaumont to serve on the staff of General J.H. Wilson, commander of the Third Cavalry Division of the Army of the Potomac. At this command, Beaumont took part in the Battle of White Oak Swamp and several skirmishes around the city of Petersburg (which was under siege by Federal troops at the time). He also participated in the raid and destruction of the Confederate Danville and Southside Railroad, as well as in the operations against Confederate troops in the Shenandoah Valley.

In October of 1864, the division was ordered to serve with the western armies. Soon after, Beaumont was appointed adjutant general of the Cavalry Corps of the Military Division of the Mississippi. While serving in this capacity, he participated in General William T. Sherman's famous "March to the Sea," being present at the battles of Nashville, Hollow Tree Gap, Richland Creek, Little River, Pulaski, Montevallo, Ebenezer Church, Selma, and the capture of Montgomery, Columbus, and Macon, Georgia.

On December 17, 1864, Beaumont was ordered to charge a Confederate artillery battery at Harpeth's River, Tennessee. He led his men in the charge (men of the 4th U.S. Cavalry) and drove the enemy away, capturing the guns and taking several prisoners. At Selma, Alabama, in April of 1865, Beaumont again displayed his bravery by leading men of the 4th Cavalry in a gallant charge of the enemy's position, resulting in victory. When the war ended in May, 1865, Beaumont remained in Georgia in command of several hundred men. It was at Macon where he received Confederate President Jefferson Davis as a prisoner.

In April of 1866 he was returned to the regular army rank of captain and took command of Troop A, 4th U.S. Cavalry, then stationed at San Antonio, Texas. From 1866 to 1875, he took part in several skirmishes with the Comanche Indians and captured 1,700 horses and mules, wiping out several camps. Because of his valuable experience, Beaumont was assigned to teach cavalry tactics at the military academy at West Point, New York. He served as an instructor from 1875 to 1879, but the call of the frontier was too strong, and he returned as a major following the death of his wife in April of 1879. From 1879 to 1888 he took part in several expeditions into New Mexico and Arizona, accomplishing his mission each time. In December of 1883, he married Maria L. Orton, the daughter of a Lawrenceville, Pennsylvania, doctor.

From 1888 to 1892 he was detailed as inspector-general for the depot of Texas. In January of 1892, he was promoted to lieutenant colonel of the 3rd U.S. Cavalry, where he again performed his duty with the precision of a professional soldier. In May of that year, Beaumont requested that he be officially retired from the service. His request was granted, and he returned home to Wilkes-Barre.

On March 30, 1898, just as the tensions of the Spanish-American War were mounting, Beaumont was awarded the Congressional Medal of Honor for gallantry at the battles of Harpeth River, Tennessee, and Selma, Alabama. After the death of his second wife, he married her sister, Stella Orton Rusling, a widow, in September of 1905. Beaumont enjoyed his retirement with his new wife for another eleven years, involving himself in several associations such as: Military Order of the Loyal Legion; Society of the Army of the Potomac; Society of the Sixth Corps; Grand Army of the Republic; Wyoming Historical and Geological Society (also known as the Luzerne County Historical Society); and the Westmoreland Club. Beaumont died on July 17, 1916, in his Wilkes-Barre home. He was interred at the Hollenback Cemetery next to the remains of his first wife, Margaret Rutter. Their marker is located about fifteen feet from the grave of another Medal of Honor Winner, Margaret's brother, James M. Rutter.

Gone But Not Forgotten | *Civil War Veterans of Northeastern Pennsylvania*

Lieutenant Colonel Eugene B. Beaumont, Staff, 4th U.S. Cavalry Regiment
Credit: U.S. Army Military History Institute Collection

Eugene B. Beaumont, Hollenback Cemetery, Wilkes-Barre

James May Rutter
May 13, 1841 – November 23, 1907

James May Rutter was born the youngest son to Nathaniel and Mary Ann Rutter at Wilkes-Barre, Pennsylvania. Nathaniel was a leader in the business community and provided for his family quite well. He was president of Miner's Savings Bank and the Hollenback Coal Company, as well as serving as the director of Vulcan Iron Works. He also served on the Wilkes-Barre City council for some time.

After completing a basic education, the young Rutter was apprenticed to a local company to learn the machinist's trade. He finished his training on May 13, 1862, his twenty-first birthday. By all rights, he should have begun a promising career as a machinist, but the excitement of military glory appealed to him more. He learned of the recruitment of a local regiment, the 143rd Pennsylvania Volunteer Infantry Regiment, and hurried to join. When Rutter reached the training ground of the regiment at Camp Luzerne on August 4, he was accepted as a private of Company C. When the regiment was mustered in on August 27, his Captain, George N. Reichard, promoted Rutter to the rank of fifth Sergeant.

The regiment trained at Camp Luzerne until November 7, then was transferred to Harrisburg where it received Enfield rifled muskets. From there the regiment was assigned to the I Corps under Major General John F. Reynolds. Colonel Edmund L. Dana, a Mexican War veteran and prominent Wilkes-Barre lawyer, commanded the regiment.

Rutter's regiment participated in the Battle of Chancellorsville in May, 1863, sustaining casualties. However, the Battle of Gettysburg on July 1, was to be the greatest test for the regiment, and for Rutter. The 143rd was one of the first infantry regiments to reach the field at Gettysburg and its duty was to hold the ground north of town long enough for Federal reinforcements to take the field. The 143rd and other regiments of the bucktail brigade were vastly outnumbered by oncoming Confederate forces and took heavy casualties. The corps, with Major General Reynolds killed, was forced to withdraw back through Gettysburg to Cemetery Ridge, south of town. It was during this retreat that Rutter would face his greatest test.

During the retreat, the commander of Rutter's company, Captain Reichard, was wounded by Confederate fire. Lieutenant John C. Kropp called out to the men of Company C to attempt a rescue of the fallen Captain, who was now lying between battle lines. There was no answer, until Sergeant James Rutter ran to the Captain's rescue under heavy Confederate fire. Rutter carried Reichard to safety but became separated from his regiment, which was forced to retreat

southward. James placed Captain Reichard in a private residence and searched for a surgeon throughout town at great risk, but could find none. He rejoined his regiment at Cemetery Ridge and found rest in a cemetery that night. At roll call the next day, Lieutenant Kropp was delighted to see him because he had given him up for dead. On July 3, the 143rd assisted with the repulse of the now famous "Pickett's Charge" which culminated in a great Northern victory.

For his bravery, Rutter was presented with a new medal being issued by Congress. He was awarded the Medal of Honor later that year for his meritorious service in action at Gettysburg on July 1, 1863. He had risked his life for his captain and was recognized for it. The medal issued to Rutter is currently held in the collections of the Luzerne County Historical Society.

Following the Battle of Gettysburg, Rutter was detailed with twenty other men to a signal station near Culpeper, Virginia. He was impressed with the duties of the signalmen and was granted a transfer to the Signal Corps in March, 1864. As a signalman, superior officers gave him commendations for his bravery in action and military bearing. He served in this capacity until June 27, 1865, when he was mustered out of service.

Rutter returned home to Wilkes-Barre a hero. He married Martha Burdett of New York, on October 16, 1866, and the couple had four children: Ellen, Frances, Nathaniel, and Augusta. Following the death of Martha in 1883, Rutter married Alvaretta Wildoner, of Shickshinny, Pennsylvania, who was fifteen years his junior. Together the couple had two children; Miriam Alvaretta in 1887 and James May Jr. in 1888. Alvaretta was the daughter of George Wildoner, a private in Company F of the same regiment in which Rutter had served, the 143rd Pennsylvania Volunteer Infantry Regiment. The grave of George Wildoner was located by the author at the Pine Hill Cemetery in Shickshinny, Pennsylvania.

Rutter worked in various career fields following his military service. He was president and assistant engineer of the Wilkes-Barre Fire Department; a surveyor with the Geological Survey of 1874; owned and operated a Wilkes-Barre hardware store; and was president of the Wilkes-Barre School Board. Following his retirement in 1888, Rutter found many duties to occupy his time. He was a charter member of the Conyngham Post No. 97 of the Grand Army of the Republic (Union veterans' organization); was a member of Masonic Lodge No. 442 of Wilkes-Barre; and was also a member of the Westmoreland Club in Wilkes-Barre.

On November 23, 1907, at the age of sixty-six, James M. Rutter died at his home on Carey Avenue in Wilkes-Barre, Pennsylvania. His remains were interred at the Hollenback Cemetery in that same city where his grave can be found today. James Rutter was a true hero who was awarded our nation's highest military honor.

The grave of Captain George N. Reichard, the man who was saved by Rutter, can also be found at the Hollenback Cemetery. Reichard went on to become lieutenant colonel of the 143rd and became a valuable and inspirational leader. Lieutenant John C. Kropp's grave can also be found at the same cemetery. Unfortunately, he was killed at the Battle of the Wilderness on May 5, 1864. The grave of the colonel of the 143rd, Edmund L. Dana, can likewise be found at the Hollenback Cemetery.

Gone But Not Forgotten | *Civil War Veterans of Northeastern Pennsylvania*

Sergeant James M. Rutter, Co.C, 143RD Pennsylvania Volunteer Infantry
Credit: Reprinted with permission of the Times Leader Newspaper

James M. Rutter, Hollenback Cemetery, Wilkes-Barre
Credit: Kristen Lindbuchler Photo

JAMES POST
1835 – November 11, 1891

On May 31, 1864, James Post, a young second lieutenant from Shickshinny, Pennsylvania, found himself huddling inside the confines of a Confederate prison at Macon, Georgia. He had been captured at the Battle of North Anna a week earlier while leading his company in battle. His unit was Company F of the 149th Pennsylvania Volunteer Infantry Regiment.

In 1862, the youthful-looking Post enlisted at Shickshinny in the Huntingdon Valley Rifles (Company F) at the age of twenty-seven. At that time he was an inexperienced, green private who perhaps thought he could take on the whole rebel army single-handedly. A year earlier, Post had married a local woman, Carrie Blanchard, at Plymouth, Pennsylvania. Now, duty called and Post left his young wife to serve his country.

Upon enlistment, Post and the company were attached to the 149th, which had been recruited from around the Commonwealth. The regiment would be a part of the famous "bucktail brigade." The brigade wore a distinctive badge on their forage caps: the severed tail of a whitetail deer. The original bucktail regiment (42nd Pennsylvania Infantry) had served with great distinction in the early years of the war as sharpshooters and skirmishers (men placed out in front of the main body of troops for the purpose of scouting the enemy position).

The regiment was led by Colonel Roy Stone, a veteran bucktail leader, and was sent to Washington for training. Once there, it was brigaded with the 143rd and 150th Pennsylvania Infantries. The brigade was drilled by Colonel Stone and attached to the I Corps, Army of the Potomac, and sent to the field in February of 1863. By this time, Post was promoted to the rank of first sergeant because of his knowledge of drill, and his military bearing. At the Battle of Chancellorsville in May, the regiment fought bravely and sustained a loss of only one man.

On July 1, 1863, the regiment sustained its greatest losses of the war at Gettysburg, Pennsylvania. The brigade was given the task of holding off an aggressive Confederate force that was increasing in numbers by the hour. The I Corps was outnumbered and flanked in the fighting, but was able to hold off the enemy for a few precious hours while Union forces were brought north to Gettysburg to meet the foe. During the heavy fighting on the McPherson farm, the 149th fought a stubborn fight, but paid the price for it, by losing 336 men and its colors that day. First Sergeant Post was injured by a spent Confederate bullet during the retreat of the Corps. He was removed to a Union field hospital where his wound was dressed.

Post returned to the regiment in the fall and spent the winter in camp with his comrades. In February, 1864, Post was given a commission and made a second lieutenant of Company F.

The I Corps was dissolved that winter and made a part of the V Corps. The 149th was assigned to the 4th division and was heavily engaged in the Battle of the Wilderness in May of 1864. In the confused, chaotic battle, the 149th lost 215 men, almost half being captured by the enemy. It again lost men (about one hundred) a few days later at the Battle of Spotsylvania on May 8-12.

The 149th engaged in another battle at the North Anna River on May 23. It had crossed the river in the evening and was advancing into nearby woods to make camp for the night when it was suddenly attacked by Confederate troops. Cooper's Battery B, of the 1st Pennsylvania Light Artillery assisted the regiment in the fighting with great skill, but the enemy was too strong, and the regiment was forced to pull back with four killed, sixteen wounded, and ten prisoners taken. One of those ten was Post, captured as he commanded his company in the fight.

Post was sent to Richmond, the Confederate capital, and then to Macon, Georgia, on May 31. There he remained a prisoner for the next ten months, suffering the hardships of a prisoner-of-war in the Confederacy. At home in Shickshinny, Carrie Post suffered the anguish of a distraught wife, unable to help her husband as he remained in the hands of his enemy. Horror stories about the infamous conditions of the Confederate prison at Andersonville, Georgia, must have added to her worry.

Post survived and was exchanged at Northeast Ferry, North Carolina, on March 1, 1865, just as the war was coming to an end. He was sent back to his regiment, which had since been detailed to act as prison guards at Elmira, New York. The former prisoner then became the prison guard. He was promoted to first lieutenant on March 29, and was sent home to his young wife for fifteen days' leave on April 26, seventeen days after Confederate General Robert E. Lee surrendered his army at Appomattox.

Post was again promoted, this time to the rank of captain, on May 27, 1865, and was mustered out of the army on June 24. He returned home to Shickshinny where he lived a happy and fulfilling life, raising a daughter, Cora, and collecting a pension of $8 per month for his disabilities. The prisoner turned prison guard died at the family home in Shickshinny on November 11, 1891, at the young age of fifty-six. He was buried in the Pine Hill Cemetery where he remains today. Carrie joined her beloved soldier on February 14, 1915.

Gone But Not Forgotten | *Civil War Veterans of Northeastern Pennsylvania*

Captain James Post, Co. F, 149th Pennsylvania Volunteer Infantry
Credit: U.S. Army Military History Institute Collection

JAMES POST, PINE HILL CEMETERY, SHICKSHINNY
CREDIT: RYAN LINDBUCHLER PHOTO

LANSFORD FOSTER CHAPMAN
November 2, 1834 – May 2, 1863

The long, bloody Civil War was finally over. Many heroes from both North and South, lay buried in the sod of numerous battlefields throughout the South. Abraham Lincoln was assassinated in April, 1865, and the nation was beginning the arduous task of healing the wounds of war, both physically and psychologically. Many veterans returned to their families in 1865, some with missing limbs, and all bearing the horrid memories of the terror and confusion of battle. They were the lucky ones. Many families sent their sons, brothers, and husbands off to war, never to see them alive again.

One such family lived in the town of Mauch Chunk, Carbon County, in 1865. Olive Jackson Chapman saw her husband off to war in 1861, learning two years later that he had fallen in battle and was among the killed. Her husband, Lansford F. Chapman, was born on a cold November day to Joseph and Martha Chapman, both of English descent. He was the eldest son and was educated in the public schools of Mauch Chunk. At the age of fifteen he began learning the trade of an engineer and worked his way up to head engineer, leading the crew that was hired to construct the Lehigh Valley Railroad from 1853 to 1854. In 1856, he married Olive, the daughter of a Carbondale physician, and the couple had two children. Their son Joseph was born in January, 1859, and daughter Hattie was born in February, 1860.

When the Civil War broke out in 1861, Chapman was a prominent engineering contractor, living in Mauch Chunk. Seeing his responsibility as a community leader, he helped recruit the "Mauch Chunk Rangers," which would later become Company E of the 28th Pennsylvania Volunteer Infantry Regiment. He was made captain and was commissioned on June 25, 1861, only three months after Confederate forces fired on the Federal garrison at Fort Sumter, South Carolina, setting off the war. The twenty-six year old engineer was a large man for the period at 6' tall (5'8" was the average height). He was listed as having a dark complexion, gray eyes, and brown hair. His younger brother Charles, also an engineer, joined the company as a second lieutenant.

Chapman left behind his wife and two small children when the company moved out to be attached to the rest of the regiment in June, 1861. Hattie, his daughter, was not yet two and would never remember her father. The regiment was raised by a wealthy Pennsylvanian, John W. Geary, who later ascended to the governership of Pennsylvania after the war. It was a large regiment, having fifteen companies, five of which would later be detached to form the nucleus of the 147th Pennsylvania Infantry in 1862. It was equipped with gray uniforms at first, later to be exchanged for the standard union blue by 1862. The regiment trained in Philadelphia and was transferred to the front at Harper's Ferry, Virginia, where it secured various points of importance, such as ferries, roads, railroads, and canals. Here the regiment fought several skirmishes and performed admirably, routing the enemy each time. It was engaged several times between October, 1861 and April, 1862, including Bolivar Heights, Louden Heights, Waterford, Leesburg, Snickersville, Upperville, Linden, and Front Royal.

Chapman led his company bravely, proving that he was an effective leader, resulting in a good reputation and making him very popular with his men. In June, 1862, he returned to Mauch Chunk on eight days' leave to distribute money to the families of the men in the company. In August, the regiment fought again at Cedar Mountain and Second Bull Run, losing a few men. The 28th next met the enemy in the bloody battle of Antietam on September 17, taking part in the savage fighting around the Dunker Church. The regiment lost 266 men that day while capturing two enemy artillery pieces and five Confederate battle flags. Captain Chapman was among the wounded that day, having suffered a wound in the abdomen by a piece of Confederate shell. His wound was not very serious and he was placed back on duty in time to command the company near Harper's Ferry once again, where the 28th engaged Confederate cavalry at Wheatland, capturing a large number of prisoners and equipment.

In October of 1862, the regiment was attached to the newly formed XII Corps, Army of the Potomac, where its brigade commander was its old regimental commander, John W. Geary. In December, the regiment was recalled to the army under General Ambrose Burnside, and was detailed to act as garrison troops at Dumfries. On December 17, the garrison was attacked by Confederate cavalry under J.E.B. Stuart and repulsed the enemy, routing it at Occoquan. The regiment spent winter camp at Aquia, where it fortified the encampment and drove off another Confederate cavalry attack.

On January 22, 1863, Chapman was promoted to major and officially took command of the regiment. Due to attrition, the staff of the regiment was severely depleted, and Chapman had been serving as its leader in the several months leading up to his promotion. In February, Chapman returned home on a ten day leave. This was the last time he would see his young wife and their two children. He returned to his regiment, concentrating on drill. According to Bates' _History of Pennsylvania Volunteers_,

> …Major L.F. Chapman, who was then in command of the regiment, and (who) was one of the most heroic and efficient officers in the army. After the promotion of Colonel Geary, Major Chapman took great interest in keeping up the character the regiment had acquired for its admirable drill and discipline, and to his untiring exertions in this regard is owing much of its subsequent fame. (Volume I, 429)

Major Chapman led his regiment in the Battle of Chancellorsville on May 1, 1863. On the first day, the 28th was ordered to charge an enemy column. As the men went forward, Chapman took a position at the head of the regiment, inspiring his men to be brave. As the regiment sprang forward with a yell, an enemy musket ball struck Chapman in the heart, killing him instantly. The next day, the 28th was ordered to construct breastworks to defend its position. There were no spades, shovels, or axes, so the men used tin cups, plates, and eating utensils. The regiment numbered three-hundred men and took part in a disastrous rear-guard action that resulted in casualties of over one-third of their number. Before the men reluctantly fell back, Chapman's brother Charles (then a first lieutenant of Company E), and a few men, buried their beloved leader on the field, plainly marking his grave.

His remains lay in the soil of Virginia for two years. In May, 1865, after hostilities had ceased, the Chapman family had his remains exhumed and returned to Mauch Chunk where they lie today. Following the funeral, Chapman's wife, Olive, was honored when the veterans of Mauch Chunk named G.A.R. Post 61 in honor of her brave husband.

Gone But Not Forgotten | *Civil War Veterans of Northeastern Pennsylvania*

Major Lansford F. Chapman, Staff, 28th Pennsylvania Volunteer Infantry
Credit: Ron Beifuss Collection

RYAN LINDBUCHLER

LANSFORD F. CHAPMAN, MAUCH CHUNK CEMETERY, JIM THORPE
CREDIT: KRISTEN LINDBUCHLER PHOTO

Samuel N. Callender
1847 – 1920

On March 8, 1864, a youthful-looking man entered the recruiting station at Easton, Pennsylvania. Based upon the photograph of Samuel Callender, there must have been some concern by the recruiting officer. The Army regulations of the period specifically stated that one had to be at least eighteen years old in order to enlist in the Army. The boy gave a scrap of paper to the officer to prove that he was eighteen and able to serve in the U.S. Army. The paper had one paragraph scribbled upon it, and was written by Newell Callender, his father, and attested to the fact that he was indeed eighteen. This note is available for inspection at the National Archives in Washington, D.C.

Callender's motivation for joining the Army in 1864 is unknown. Perhaps he was inspired by patriotism, but one can suppose that the $300 bounty that the government was offering might have been an influence. Callender was mustered into service as a private of Company L, 2nd Pennsylvania Heavy Artillery. On the muster rolls he is listed as having gray eyes, light hair, a fair complexion, and 5'4" tall. A scar on the left side of his neck was also noted. He was listed as being born in Luzerne County and a farmer by trade. According to his father's note, the family farm was located near Factoryville, Pennsylvania.

When Callender reached the regiment in the next few weeks, changes occurred. Since there was a large number of men filling the ranks of the regiment, it was too large to serve as one regiment (in April it held about 3,300 men). The regiment was split in two and Company L was assigned to the new regiment, named the Second Provisional Heavy Artillery. Heavy artillery regiments were meant to man very large artillery pieces that were usually mounted inside fortifications. However, during the war, they were trained in infantry tactics and sometimes acted as infantry units. When Ulysses S. Grant took command of Union armies, he ordered most heavy artillery regiments to be attached to infantry brigades. According to Army regulations, an infantry regiment was to consist of about one thousand men. By 1862, because of the high rate of casualties, the average infantry regiment numbered about 200 to 300 men. This did not occur with the heavy artillery regiments because the rate of attrition was very low because they spent the first three years of the war inside fortifications, rarely under fire.

Callender was part of the 2nd Provisional Heavy Artillery when it was attached to the IX Army Corps under General Ambrose Burnside in April, 1864. The regiment acted as a rather large infantry regiment and surprised the veterans of the old, beat-up, and hard fought infantry

regiments who sometimes mistook the large regiment for an entire brigade. The regiment took part in the battles of the Wilderness, Spotsylvania, Cold Harbor, and the North Anna River, where it suffered significant casualties.

On June 17, 1864, the regiment was ordered to charge Confederate fortifications at Petersburg. The regiment charged valiantly, but lost 246 men as a result of an uncoordinated attack along the front. The position was too strong to capture, and the men withdrew to Union lines. Callender took part in the charge and returned unhurt.

Over the next few months, the regiment took part in the siege of Petersburg and was part of the attacking force on July 30, 1864. The 48th Pennsylvania Volunteer Infantry Regiment, made up of Schuylkill County coal miners, had dug a mine under Confederate fortifications and filled the mine with thousands of pounds of gunpowder. When the mine exploded, the attacking force, made up partly of the 2nd Provisional Heavy Artillery, was to charge through the breach in the Confederate line, dislodging the enemy. The action was a disaster because there was a long delay before the order was given, and the attacking force was lead **into** the crater, and not **around** it. When the men charged into the crater, they had no ladders to climb out and were massacred by Confederate troops as a result. The regiment lost many men that day, but Callender again remained unscathed.

The regiment fought at Weldon Railroad in August and numbered only about four hundred men when it was rejoined with the original 2nd Pennsylvania Heavy Artillery on September 5, 1864. It had lost well over half of its effective strength (about one thousand men) in the months of service it had performed. With the XVIII Corps, the regiment again faced the enemy at Fort Gilmer on September 29 and met again with disaster, losing over two hundred men and the commanding officer (Major James L. Anderson).

In January, 1865, the term of service of the regiment was up, but enough of the men re-enlisted in order to continue the existence of the regiment. Because Callender had enlisted for a period of three years, he had to remain in service with the regiment. The 2nd again charged Confederate earthworks around Petersburg on March 31, 1865, and were successful, taking many prisoners. When the city fell to Union forces soon after, the regiment was detailed to act as an occupying force until the close of the war in mid April. After the surrender of the Confederate Army of Northern Virginia, the regiment was broken up by company and distributed throughout the southern counties of Virginia to maintain law and order there. Callender was mustered out of the service with the rest of the regiment on January 29, 1866.

He returned to northeast Pennsylvania to resume life as a farmer. He died in 1920 and was buried in the Dunmore Cemetery, where his remains lie today.

Gone But Not Forgotten | *Civil War Veterans of Northeastern Pennsylvania*

Private Samuel N. Callender, Co. L, 2ND Pennsylvania Heavy Artillery
Credit: G.A.R. Post 139 Collection

Samuel Callender, about 1885
Credit: G.A.R. Post 139 Collection

STEPHEN GREGORY
July 16, 1849 – July 31, 1935

By August, 1864, the war had been raging for three years at the cost of hundreds of thousands of lives. Many citizens of the north were growing tired of sending their sons, brothers, and husbands to fight in a war that at times seemed hopeless. President Lincoln, along with Congress, had instituted the draft years before, and some men had no choice but to serve the union cause. Fate chose a relatively wealthy Luzerne County man named John Gurver to serve as a soldier for the United States Army when his name was chosen in the draft.

Gurver was unwilling to serve in this capacity and choose to hire a substitute to serve in his place. Federal law allowed citizens to do this, as long as they paid the substitute an agreeable bounty. In the North, this exemption fueled opposition to the war by those in the majority who could not afford such a luxury and were forced to serve in the military themselves. It is not known how Gurver was able to find a substitute, but it is most likely that he took an advertisement out in a local newspaper.

On August 31, 1864, a fifteen-year-old boy, Stephen Gregory, appeared before the recruiting officer at Scranton, Pennsylvania, to serve in place of Gurver. Gregory had the permission of his parents to enlist, and took the oath to serve in Company B of the 58th Pennsylvania Volunteer Infantry Regiment. It is not known how much Gurver paid Gregory to serve as his substitute, but it was probably several hundred dollars. Contemporaries describe Gregory as having blue eyes, light hair, a light complexion, and being 5' 8" in height. Gregory was born in Union Township on the farm of his parents, Abraham and Sarah. There he spent his first fifteen years learning the skills needed to run a farm. He attended the Reyburn School to the eighth grade, and could barely read and write. Perhaps as a boy he learned about the fate of his great-great grandfather, Elijah Richards, who was a soldier of the 24th Connecticut Militia Regiment in the American Revolution. Richards was killed in the Wyoming Massacre of 1778.

Gregory joined a regiment that saw many hard fought campaigns through the first three years of the war, principally serving in the deep south against southern coastal fortifications and port cities. It was sent north in the spring of 1864 to serve in Virginia with the XVIII Corps, where it fought at Cold Harbor and the siege of Petersburg. In July, the veterans of the regiment were sent home for furlough and to recruit men to fill the depleted ranks. It was during this time that Gregory was enlisted into Company B and was transported with the other new recruits to Virginia to join the rest of the 58th at Petersburg. Gregory, along with the rest of the regiment, was issued the model 1861 Springfield musket and took his place in the company. It was not long before the boy-turned-soldier would participate in his first battle.

In September, the 58th, along with the 188th Pennsylvania Infantry, received orders to lead an infantry charge across open ground against Confederate held Fort Harrison in the Petersburg defensive works. This would be a test of courage for the veterans of the regiment and a terrifying ordeal for recruits such as Gregory, who had never seen the face of battle before. The mission of the regiment was to capture the fort, along with as many prisoners as possible. The area over which the assault was made was open ground extending about 1,800 yards. The open ground provided little protection for the men. Fort Harrison held hundreds of infantrymen with small arms and over fifteen artillery pieces, capable of inflicting heavy casualties on any attacking force.

The regiment bravely marched toward the fort at a normal marching pace. As they approached, enemy artillery began to fire upon them, hurling hundreds of projectiles at the men, tearing great holes in their ranks, killing and maiming dozens. They made their approach in a calm and military manner, as if they were simply drilling in camp on an autumn afternoon. As they came about five hundred yards from the fort, they received rifle fire as well, causing additional casualties. At this location, the regiment found a small rise in the ground and the men immediately fell to the ground for some form of cover. It was here that the men, including Gregory, gathered their courage, stood up with a scream and made a mad rush toward the fort, scaling the parapets and driving the Confederate defenders to the rear in terror. The 228 man regiment lost six officers and 128 men (over fifty percent), including three color-bearers. Private Stephen Gregory was one of the lucky ones who survived unhurt and probably felt a great sense of accomplishment coming through his first battle with his honor and courage intact. He had indeed gone into the battle a boy, and came out a man.

That same day, the regiment was ordered to make another attack on Confederate works at the Star Fort. The regiment captured several cannons and inflicted serious damage on the enemy before being forced to withdraw to Fort Harrison when reinforcements failed to arrive. The following day Confederate forces assaulted the fort but were repulsed by the men of the 58th with heavy losses. The remainder of the year the regiment built roads and constructed earthworks and rifle pits.

The 58th regiment participated in the closing campaign in the spring, 1865, pursuing Robert E. Lee to Appomattox Court House, where the war came to an end on April 9. Gregory, though not even sixteen years of age, was a grizzled veteran of the U.S. Army and was discharged on June 12, 1865, after the Union troops under William T. Sherman had received the surrender of the only remaining Confederate army in May. Gregory returned home to his father's farm in Union Township soon after and settled down to life as a farmer in northeastern Pennsylvania.

In December of 1869, Gregory, now twenty, married a local woman, Frances Bilby, and the couple was blessed with ten children during the course of their long marriage. Gregory remained a farmer his entire life, but supplemented his income by becoming a stone mason, eventually creating his own contracting business. In 1911, he received a pension from the government for rheumatism and neuralgia (loss of nerve function) that he had contracted while in the service of his country.

In November of 1927, his wife Frances died. Eight years later, the eighty six-year-old Civil War veteran had a stroke and passed away on July 31, 1935. He was laid to rest at the Sorber Cemetery in Reyburn, Pennsylvania, alongside his beloved wife. Stephen Gregory is another good example of the citizen soldier of northeastern Pennsylvania who did his duty for the Union.

Gone But Not Forgotten | *Civil War Veterans of Northeastern Pennsylvania*

Private Stephen Gregory, Co. B, 58th Pennsylvania Volunteer Infantry
Credit: Stephen B. Killian – descendant photo

Stephen Gregory, Sorber Cemetery, Reyburn
Credit: Ryan Lindbuchler Photo

Thomas C. Harkness
1823 – November 30, 1882

Not much is known about the early life of Thomas Harkness. He was born in Scotland in 1823 and immigrated to the United States at about the age of twenty-seven, along with his wife Agnes, who was also Scottish. He was employed as a mining superintendent by 1860 and was living in Wilkes-Barre, Pennsylvania, when the Civil War began in 1861. The couple had four children, all born in Pennsylvania, when Harkness decided to serve his adopted country in the midst of a savage civil war. Perhaps he thought it would be a quick and decisive victory for the North, but he would soon find out otherwise.

Possibly because of his leadership experience as a coal mining superintendent, he was mustered into U.S. service as a captain of Company H, 81st Pennsylvania Volunteer Infantry Regiment. Company H was made up of men from Carbon County who had predominately been mine laborers in the coalfields of the Commonwealth. The 81st was recruited by James Miller, a Mexican War veteran, and was composed mostly of Philadelphia men. Companies G, H, and I were from Carbon County and K was from Luzerne County.

Harkness led his company through the thickest of the fighting in the East with the II Corps of the Army of the Potomac. A few of his men helped carry the body of the slain Colonel Miller from the field at Fair Oaks in May of 1862, and Captain Harkness was called upon to temporarily lead the regiment in the confusion of the fighting there. His military prowess was utilized when Harkness was chosen to lead reconnaissance details to feel out enemy positions during McClellan's Peninsula Campaign. He did an excellent job and was commended by his superiors.

The regiment was heavily engaged at Yorktown, White Oak Swamp, Savage Station, Glendale, and Charles City Crossroads. It was at the last that the regiment took part in savage night fighting in which Colonel Johnson was wounded, along with Captain Harkness and many other 81st men. During the fighting, Harkness was struck by enemy rifle fire and shrapnel four times. He was forced to retire from the field after becoming too weak from a severe loss of blood.

Harkness recovered from his wounds and returned to Company H just in time to lead it at the Battle of Antietam on September 17, 1862. He survived that fight unharmed and was promoted to major in November of that year. The Battle of Fredericksburg in December was a catastrophe for the newly nicknamed "Chippewa Regiment." Out of the 261 men of the regiment that assaulted the fortified enemy position on Marye's Heights, 176 were casualties. One of these casualties

was Major Harkness, who was the victim of an enemy minié ball. He had now spilled blood for his adopted country twice. Most men would have considered their duty done, but not the fighting Scotsman named Harkness. He returned to the regiment by the Spring, 1863 and was promoted to the rank of lieutenant colonel on April 7.

On May 3, 1863 the regiment was engaged with the enemy at the Battle of Chancellorsville. The II Corps (which the 81st was part of) was given the duty of acting as a rear-guard for the retreating Army of the Potomac. The regiment performed this service valiantly and took considerable losses. Lieutenant Colonel Harkness again spilled blood for the Union and was counted among the wounded. He was again seriously wounded by an enemy musket ball and was carried from the field by his men. Harkness returned home to his family to recover, hoping that he might be strong enough to return to the regiment and serve it once more.

He returned to the regiment at its winter quarters near Brandy Station in the fall of 1863. The 81st, depleted in numbers from hard campaigning, was able to recruit new soldiers and was virtually brought back to full strength by Spring, 1864. Lieutenant Colonel Harkness was instrumental in training these new men, and looked forward to leading the newly recognized "veteran volunteers" in the field under the command of the newly appointed Ulysses S. Grant. Unfortunately, Harkness was too disabled to do so and was forced to resign his commission before the regiment took the field in May, 1864.

Harkness returned to his young family at Wilkes-Barre and resumed his career as a mining contractor. Together the couple had three additional children and led a comfortable life in Wilkes-Barre. At the age of fifty-nine, the six-time wounded lieutenant colonel of the "Chippewa Regiment" died at his home in Wilkes-Barre. Harkness is a shining example of those immigrants who came to America to start a new life and felt a compelling sense of duty to the Union and their newly adopted nation.

Thomas C. Harkness was laid to rest at the Hollenback Cemetery in Wilkes-Barre, along with his wife Agnes and several of his children. Not thirty yards from his gravesite lie the remains of another member of the 81st, First Sergeant Hugh Blair of Company H, who was recruited into the regiment by Captain Harkness.

Gone But Not Forgotten | *Civil War Veterans of Northeastern Pennsylvania*

Lieutenant Colonel Thomas Harkness, Staff, 81st Pennsylvania Volunteer Infantry
Credit: Grace M. J. Lynch Collection

Thomas Harkness, Hollenback Cemetery, Wilkes-Barre
Credit: Kristen Lindbuchler Photo

WILLIAM F. BLOSS
February 4, 1839 – August 4, 1864

The 76th Pennsylvania Volunteer Infantry Regiment was being raised in August of 1861, following the defeat of Union forces at the battle of First Bull Run on July 21. The 76th was known as the "Keystone Zouaves," and was being raised predominantly in western and southern Pennsylvania. A Zouave regiment was much like other Federal regiments, except that the men wore very intricate uniforms patterned after French troops who had been fighting on the continent of Africa in the years preceding the Civil War. During this period the French were considered the trendsetters of military fashion, and many Americans wanted to mirror this style in the U.S. Army. The 76th adopted the Zouave pattern uniform, including a fancy navy blue jacket trimmed in red, accompanied by a sky blue baggy pair of Arab-style trousers, and a sky blue tasseled fez.

When recruiting officers of the 76th entered Scranton to recruit men for Company H, local men swarmed to wear the dashing uniform of a Pennsylvania Zouave. One of those men was William Bloss. He enlisted on September 11, 1861 at Scranton as a private. On muster rolls he was listed as being 5'9" tall, having gray eyes, sandy hair, and a fair complexion. The twenty-two year-old carpenter turned soldier set out with the regiment, leaving his mother Sarah and sister Sophia behind. His father, William, had left years earlier, abandoning his young son, daughter, and wife.

The new regiment reached Fortress Monroe on the Virginia coast in November, received its new colors, and was transferred to Hilton Head, South Carolina. The regiment would spend the majority of its term of service in the deep South with the X Corps, aiding the Union cause by attempting to capture Confederate coastal fortifications and cities on the east coast. Its first duties consisted of building fortifications and drilling at Hilton Head. This was performed through the remainder of 1861 until the following spring. Bloss's leadership abilities were recognized early, and in February of 1862, he was promoted to first sergeant of his company.

The regiment met the enemy in battle for the first time in an attack on Charleston, South Carolina, on June 16, 1862. The attack was disastrous, and the regiment was forced to fall back without taking the Confederate positions. On October 22, Bloss was again promoted, this time to the rank of second lieutenant of Company H. On the same day, the regiment was ordered to attack Confederate positions on the Pocotaligo River. This attack was well done, but the positions were too strong, and the regiment was forced to again fall back, losing seventy-five men.

The regiment next made another ill-fated attack in July of 1863 at Fort Wagner, South Carolina. The fort protected Charleston Harbor, and its capture was essential in order to capture the city. In the days preceding the attack, the 76th was transferred to Strong's brigade, which included the now famous 54th Massachusetts Colored Infantry Regiment (as portrayed in the movie *Glory*). On the morning of July 11, the regiment charged the fort, with General Strong leading the charge. Again, the regiment was cut down in the attack, losing 187 men. Another charge was made on the evening July 18, with the 54th Massachusetts leading the charge. This attack was a failure, and the 76th lost seventeen more men as casualties. Bloss survived unhurt and was again promoted, this time to first lieutenant.

The regiment was pulled back to Hilton Head where it would take the next seven months to rest and recuperate. In May, 1864 the X Corps was ordered to Virginia to assist the Army of the James in the capture of Richmond. It was engaged in battle with the enemy once again at Drewry's Bluff and took a loss of sixty-five killed and wounded. In a letter to his sister, Bloss described an incident that occurred during the battle. He stated that a Confederate soldier had taken aim on him. A soldier from Company G yelled to him just in the nick of time and Bloss was able to dodge the bullet and shoot the man with his revolver. This letter is readily available for study at the National Archives in Washington, D.C. The 76th next fought at Cold Harbor in June and again took heavy casualties.

At Petersburg in July, 1864, the regiment was given the task of front line picket duty. Petersburg was under siege by Union forces because its control was essential for the capture of Richmond, the capital of the Confederacy. If Union forces could hold Petersburg, it would be nearly impossible for Confederate troops to defend Richmond. On July 23, Bloss was commanding Company H while it was on picket duty in the front line trenches near the City Point Railroad. Bloss was inside a fortified room, called a bombproof, with another officer, when an artillery shell exploded at the doorway. This explosion sent several iron shell fragments, called shrapnel, sailing in several different directions inside of the bombproof. Shrapnel struck Bloss in both legs and torso, shattering bones and puncturing organs.

Bloss's limp body was carried back through Union lines, and he was sent to Hampton Hospital at Fortress Monroe, in order to recuperate from his wounds. He never improved and died twelve days later. His personal effects were sent home to his mother and sister including the following: 1 uniform (coat, trousers, shirt), one cartridge box, one bullet mould, one sword and belt, one sash, one watch and chain, two revolvers, one pair of field glasses, three pairs of gloves, and $1.25 in cash.

Bloss's mother Sarah had his body sent home to Providence, Pennsylvania. (Luzerne County), and his remains were buried in the Dunmore Cemetery where they remain today. Sarah received a pension of $17 per month as compensation for her loss. Lieutenant William F. Bloss gave all for his country. He is among the heroes who exemplified courage, dedication to duty, and true patriotism in the midst of a bloody civil war.

Gone But Not Forgotten | *Civil War Veterans of Northeastern Pennsylvania*

Lieutenant William F. Bloss, Co. H, 76th Pennsylvania Volunteer Infantry
Credit: Pennsylvania Historical and Museum Commission Collection

William F. Bloss, Dunmore Cemetery
Credit: Ryan Lindbuchler Photo

WILSON BEERS
July 25, 1833 – August 11, 1902

Wilson Beers was born in Luzerne County and received little education as a child. When the Civil War broke out in 1861, Wilson was working as a mine laborer in the mining village of Eckley, Pennsylvania, in Luzerne County. Perhaps Beers saw a chance of escaping the hard life that came with working in the coal mines, and was eager to experience new things and possibly achieve military glory.

Beers immediately enlisted in Company I of the 6th Pennsylvania Volunteer Infantry Regiment, a ninety-day volunteer regiment. Company I was recruited at Mauch Chunk (now Jim Thorpe) by a local militia captain named Eli T. Conner. Beers would later serve under Conner when he joined a three-year regiment. The 6th saw little action under General Robert Patterson in his operation to capture the Federal arsenal at Harper's Ferry, Virginia. The 6th was mustered out in July of 1861 and Beers returned to his career as a coal mine laborer. However, he would not serve in this capacity for long.

When Captain Charles E. Foster, an Eckley native and company store clerk, began to recruit a company to serve in the 81st Pennsylvania Infantry Regiment in September of 1861, Beers wasted no time in joining. The 81st was a three-year regiment that would definitely see action. According to records, when Beers enlisted, he was 5' 3 ½", had a fair complexion, sandy hair, and gray eyes. Beers was enlisted as a private in Company K and served in that company until his discharge in 1864. Company K was made up of friends and neighbors from Eckley and other surrounding towns in southern Luzerne County.

The regiment was attached to the 1st Brigade, 1st Division, II Corps of the Army of the Potomac and was serving at the front by March, 1862. The regiment saw much action and sustained many casualties. Lieutenant Colonel Eli Conner, who had enlisted Beers into the 6th Pennsylvania Infantry, was killed, along with the original colonel, James Miller, by July, 1862. Beers was present when the regiment was engaged at Fair Oaks, Yorktown, Savage Station, White Oak Swamp, Glendale, Malvern Hill, the now famous "sunken road" at Antietam, Fredericksburg (where the regiment lost 176 men out of 261), Chancellorsville, and Gettysburg.

At Gettysburg on July 2, the 81st was rushed from the Union center to support troops from the retreating III Corps at the now famous Wheatfield. A letter was written by Corporal James Carroll of Company K on behalf of Beers, who was applying for an army pension in the 1890's. An excerpt from that letter reads:

...I knew you from the time we left Camp California in 62 and have stood beside you in many a hard fought battle. I have marched with you many a hard days march. I saw you at Cemetery Hill at Gettysburg and when we started to dubble-quick for the Wheatfield with one hand holding your cartridge box claiming you were in much distress and you afterwards told me you were ruptured. I saw you when but a few feet from you falling to the ground dead as I supposed with a ball through the neck and saw that brave little Welchman Billy Richards (Sgt., Company K) bending over you and bearing you off the field.

The "rupture" that Carroll spoke of was an inguinal hernia that had created so much pain for Beers. In addition to the rupture, Beers was hit by a musket ball in the neck during the assault in which the colorbearer of the regiment, James "Reddy" McHale, was killed. In describing his wound, Captain John W. Pryor wrote:

....(Beers) was wounded by a gun shot ball in the neck. The ball struck him just back of the right ear in the neck and passed through the chords of the neck and came out on back of the neck near the left ear.

Beers recovered from his wound and served with the regiment again at the Wilderness, Spotsylvania, Po River, Totopotomoy, North Anna, and Cold Harbor, and survived unscathed. On November 5, 1864, Beers was discharged by reason of expiration of term of service at Philadelphia, Pennsylvania.

Little is known about the life of Wilson Beers after the war. What is known is that he returned to Luzerne County and resumed work as a laborer. He received an army pension for his disability in the 1890s and moved to the Borough of Ashley, Pennsylvania, where he lived out the remainder of his life. He was married to Hattie Soden in the late 1860s and the couple had three children: Annie S. in 1869, Stanley S. in 1870, and Estella S. in 1874.

Hattie died in February of 1898 and was buried in Maple Hill Cemetery. On August 11, 1902, Wilson Beers followed her in death. He died at his home in Ashley of unknown causes. He was laid to rest beside his wife and their one-year-old son Stanley who had died in 1871. Wilson Beers is a good example of the common, everyday man from northeastern Pennsylvania who did his duty for the Union.

There is a problem, however. When engaged in the cemetery searches I was delighted to find the headstone of Wilson Beers at the Hollenback Cemetery in Wilkes-Barre, Pennsylvania. As my search of local gravesites continued, I was even more surprised to find ANOTHER headstone of Wilson Beers at the Maple Hill Cemetery in Hanover Township, Pennsylvania. It can be assumed that since his wife and child are interred at Maple Hill, he is interred there as well.

Gone But Not Forgotten | *Civil War Veterans of Northeastern Pennsylvania*

PRIVATE WILSON BEERS, CO. K, 81ST PENNSYLVANIA VOLUNTEER INFANTRY
CREDIT: JON WILSON COLLECTION

WILSON BEERS, HOLLENBACK CEMETERY, WILKES-BARRE
CREDIT: KRISTEN LINDBUCHLER PHOTO

ELI TAYLOR CONNER
March 27, 1832 – July 1, 1862

Eli T. Conner was born in Luzerne County to William and Rachel Conner. His family moved to Mauch Chunk (modern-day Jim Thorpe) soon after his birth. Unfortunately, Eli would never know his father because of the latter's untimely death in 1833. Conner was educated at Wyoming Seminary in Kingston, Pennsylvania, and then moved on as an adolescent to attend a military academy in Bristol, Pennsylvania.

As a young man, Conner was employed as a civil engineer during the construction of the Lehigh Valley Railroad and also served in North Carolina for a year as an engineer. In 1855, he married Mary Chapman Foster, also of Mauch Chunk. Two years later the young couple would have a son, William Foster Conner, in 1857, and a daughter, Rachel Louise Conner, in 1859.

In the 1850s, Conner used his military education by leading several militia companies in the area. When he and Mary lived in Summit Hill, Pennsylvania, he was elected lieutenant and later captain of the Carbon Guards, a well equipped local militia unit. When the family moved back to Mauch Chunk in the late 1850s Conner served as captain of the "Cleaver Artillerists." When this unit disbanded, he served as captain of the "Anderson Grays." His leadership skills were obviously very valuable to local volunteer militias.

When President Lincoln called for volunteers to serve in the military to put down the rebellion, Conner answered the call with much enthusiasm. He immediately helped recruit and organize three companies of infantry that would serve as ninety-day volunteers. The three companies would become A, I, and K of the 6th Pennsylvania Volunteer Infantry Regiment. Conner served as captain of Company A, formerly the "Anderson Grays."

The 6th Infantry saw little action in its ninety-day service, being attached to General Robert Patterson's command. The regiment participated in the operation to capture the Federal arsenal at Harper's Ferry, Virginia, then in Confederate hands. The regiment was disbanded and returned home to Mauch Chunk in July of 1861.

Conner returned home and was approached by James Miller, a Mexican War veteran, and local postmaster. Miller had been charged with recruiting a regiment for three years service and knew Conner was well known throughout Carbon County as a capable military officer. His reputation would draw many recruits needed to fill the ranks of the one thousand-man regiment. Miller set up recruiting headquarters at Easton, Pennsylvania, and Conner remained in Mauch Chunk to enlist recruits there and mourn the death of his wife Mary, who had died of tuberculosis on September 10. With the assistance of Charles Johnson, who recruited in Philadelphia,

the regiment reached full strength by October of 1861. Miller was commissioned colonel, Charles Johnson lieutenant colonel, and Eli Conner, major. The regiment became known as the 81st Pennsylvania Volunteer Infantry. Companies A, B, C, D, E, and F were primarily from Philadelphia. Companies G, H, and I were made up of men from Carbon County. Company K was primarily made up of men from in and around the mining village of Eckley, in southern Luzerne County.

In December of 1861, Conner received the terrible news that his four-year-old son, Willie, had suffered the same fate as his mother and died of tuberculosis. With this saddening news, Conner traveled with the regiment to the front. The regiment was attached to the 1st Brigade, 1st Division, II Corps in the Army of the Potomac, where it would remain for its entire service. The regiment received its baptism of fire at the Battle of Fair Oaks on May 30, 1862. Colonel Miller was killed while leading the regiment in action and Major Conner was promoted to lieutenant colonel.

The regiment was next engaged at the Battle of Charles City Crossroads on June 30. It was here that the regiment lost its next commander, Colonel Charles Johnson, who was wounded while leading the regiment. Command of the regiment passed to Eli T. Conner. He led the regiment throughout the remainder of the battle with great skill and efficiency. Little did he know that it would be his last day on earth.

That evening, the regiment was posted at Malvern Hill, Virginia, in order to protect the Union position there. When the enemy attacked the Federal line with great tenacity, the 81st regiment, along with the rest of the brigade, was rushed to support the line. According to Bates _History of Pennsylvania Volunteers_, "here, while leading on his men with great coolness and bravery, Lieutenant Colonel Conner was killed." The brigade bloodily repulsed every assault of the enemy and the position held.

His men lovingly buried their brave leader. His body would remain there until May 30, 1865, when friends from Mauch Chunk searched the field until his remains were found and returned to Mauch Chunk. On June 7, his remains were escorted by three companies of infantry from Tamaqua, Pennsylvania, and laid to rest next to his wife and son in the Mauch Chunk Cemetery, where they remain today. A G.A.R. (Grand Army of the Republic) post was named in his honor in 1869 in the town of Summit Hill, Pennsylvania. He was a true hero who was sadly missed by all in the community and fondly remembered by those who had served under his command.

Gone But Not Forgotten | *Civil War Veterans of Northeastern Pennsylvania*

Lieutenant Colonel Eli T. Conner, Staff, 81st Pennsylvania Volunteer Infantry
Credit: Grace M. J. Lynch Collection

Eli T. Conner, Mauch Chunk Cemetery, Jim Thorpe
Credit: Kristen Lindbuchler Photo

PATRICK DELACY
November 25, 1834 – April 27, 1915

It was the second day of the Battle of the Wilderness in May, 1864, and the two armies bloodied themselves in mortal combat, feeling their way through the dense, smoke-filled forest. The 143rd Pennsylvania Volunteer Infantry Regiment, made up of men from the northeastern portion of the Commonwealth, had fought bravely the day before, losing two most valued commanders: Colonel Edmund Dana (captured) and Lieutenant Colonel John D. Musser (killed in action on the 6th). The 143rd was attached to the V Corps and was a part of the bucktail brigade. Commanding Company A was a twenty-nine year-old first sergeant from Carbondale, Pennsylvania, named Patrick DeLacy.

On the evening of May 6, the regiment was resting near the Brock Road when the rebel yell was heard nearby. Immediately the brigade was ordered to its feet and given the order to stem the Confederate charge that was coming in its direction. The regiment advanced into a clearing, taking heavy losses from the furious Confederate gunfire in its front. Sensing hesitation by his men, Sergeant DeLacy charged between the two armies, seized the flag of a Confederate color-bearer, and shot the man down in plain view of everyone. Inspired by this valiant show of bravery, the brigade tenaciously attacked the Confederate troops and was able to stop their advance. DeLacy's actions at the Wilderness were said to ensure the success of the brigade on that part of the field.

Patrick DeLacy was born in Carbondale in 1834 to Mr. and Mrs. William DeLacy. William was a shoemaker who came to the United States in the early 1800s from Ireland and was among the earliest settlers of Carbondale. DeLacy spent his early years on the family farm, assisting his father and brother John with the work. At the age of sixteen he decided to leave the farm and make his way in the world as a man. He settled in Dunmore and began work as a grocer's clerk at the store of F.D. Collins. DeLacy was not satisfied with this line of work and decided to try his luck at coal mining. By the age of eighteen, he had had enough of the tough life that comes with being a coal miner and decided to learn the trade of a tanner and currier.

He learned the trade in Tannersville and was soon invited to work at the Jeremiah Wunder tannery in Trucksville, Pennsylvania. DeLacy boarded with the Wunders and began a courtship with Jeremiah's daughter, Rebecca. Wunder discouraged his daughter from seeing DeLacy because the Wunders were of a Protestant faith, and DeLacy was a Catholic. Nevertheless, the couple married on January 9, 1858. The young couple moved to Newark, New Jersey, then

to Pike County, Pennsylvania, and back to Luzerne County where DeLacy was able to lease a tannery.

When war broke out in 1861, DeLacy's brother, John, joined the 15th Pennsylvania Volunteer Infantry Regiment, and served his ninety days of duty. Later, he joined a New York infantry regiment that was attached to the famed Irish Brigade. DeLacy preferred to stay at home and be with his wife and young daughter for the time being. The year 1862 brought with it a panic that a Confederate Army might be invading Pennsylvania's soil. By summer, DeLacy felt it was his duty to serve his nation and his state by volunteering for service in the army.

On August 26, 1862, DeLacy joined the 143rd Pennsylvania Volunteer Infantry Regiment, with the full support of his wife. Before he left, he had a picture taken of his wife and their daughter. He took the picture with him with the intention of placing it in his pocket with a letter of instruction saying that should he be killed in battle, the person finding his body should add the details of his death and mail it to his wife. Fortunately, Rebecca never received that letter and picture.

DeLacy enlisted in Scranton as a private in Company A. The 143rd was a regiment made up mostly of Luzerne County men and saw some of the heaviest fighting of the war. The regiment trained at Camp Luzerne (modern-day Luzerne Borough) until the fall. It was then transferred ultimately south to Washington, thence to the Army of the Potomac where it was attached to the I Corps. The regiment first met the enemy at Chancellorsville in May, 1863, and performed its duty well, with Private DeLacy being promoted to sergeant by early 1863. DeLacy's officers noted that he was cool and collected during conflict with the enemy, having sound military judgment in situations where many men would crack under the stress of the situation.

In July, 1863, the regiment faced another test at the Battle of Gettysburg. There, the regiment, along with the rest of the bucktail brigade and the I Corps, held off a potent Confederate onslaught that threatened the entire Union Army. On July 1, the Corps was able to delay the Confederate advance long enough to allow the rest of the Union army to make its way north to Gettysburg and hold valuable positions south of town. The fight cost the regiment dearly, but DeLacy made it through safely.

The regiment took part in minor skirmishes that fall, and its Corps (I Corps) was dissolved because it had sustained disastrous casualties through 1863. The regiment was assigned to the V Corps, where it remained for the rest of the war. According to, _Avery Harris' Civil War Journal_, during the winter, the men of the 149th Pennsylvania Infantry challenged the men of the 143rd to a snowball fight. The regiments faced off in formation, firing volleys of snowballs at one another. The men of the 143rd were victorious, but DeLacy nearly lost an eye in the fight.

The spring campaign of 1864 opened with the Battle of the Wilderness in May. It was here that DeLacy distinguished himself not only in the taking of the Confederate battle-flag, but in an incident that occurred the day before. The Wilderness was a very confused battle in which troops were caught up in a dense forest in northern Virginia, unable to see their surroundings because of the foliage and the smoke produced by the black powder used in the weapons of the period. Regiments became separated from one another, and battle lines were easily broken. This confusion resulted in many incidents of regiments firing on their own comrades by mistake. Perhaps worst of all, forest fires began, and many wounded lay helpless on the ground, struggling to get away from the flames that were slowly creeping toward them. Many could not escape and were burned alive.

First Sergeant DeLacy held his company in position that day, but could not stand to let the

cries of the wounded in front of his company go unheeded. If he attempted to go and carry them off the field, the enemy might fire on the rescue party. As the wind slowly pushed the fire toward the dying men, DeLacy came up with a plan to fight fire with fire, as had been done at the family farm. His plan was approved, and he sent two men to perform the task. They successfully accomplished their mission, and the fire was prevented from reaching their comrades.

The regiment took part in the remainder of the battles that occurred in 1864-5, serving valiantly and taking many casualties. These battles included: Spotsylvania, North Anna, Cold Harbor, Totopotomoy, Bethesda Church, Petersburg, Weldon Railroad, Boydton Road, and Hatcher's Run. In October, 1864, DeLacy was promoted to the rank of sergeant major. This rank is the highest enlisted rank allowed in an infantry regiment of the period. The photograph included in this book provides an image of DeLacy in the uniform of a sergeant major. In February, 1865, the regiment, along with three others in the brigade, was sent north to Hart's Island, New York, to perform guard duty. This was done because the regiment had suffered so many casualties as to be too small to serve adequately in the field. Here the regiment escorted convalescents and new recruits to the front and guarded Confederate prisoners who were being held there. On May 24, DeLacy was promoted to second lieutenant of Company D. This was well over a month after Confederate General Robert E. Lee surrendered his army at Appomattox. The regiment was mustered out of service on June 12, 1865.

DeLacy returned home to Wilkes-Barre with many of his comrades as a hero. He resumed his life in the leather business, having several more children with his wife. In 1867 he was appointed Deputy U.S. Marshal and served in this capacity until he resigned in 1871. In that year, he was elected to the state legislature where he served two terms. From 1877 to 1879 he served as the Lackawanna County Auditor and was Scranton City police chief from 1879 to 1885. In 1885 he resigned as police chief and became assistant postmaster. In 1889 he was elected Seventh Ward Alderman and served in this capacity until his death in 1915.

He and his wife had twelve children, eight of whom died before reaching adulthood. DeLacy served as president of the 143rd Regimental Association for almost fifty years and was very active in the local post of the Grand Army of the Republic in Scranton. In April, 1894, he was informed that he had received the Medal of Honor for his actions at the Battle of the Wilderness in May of 1864. In April, 1915, the local soldier-hero passed away at his home near Scranton and was buried in the Moscow Cemetery where one may visit his remains today.

Sergeant Major Patrick Delacy, Staff, 143RD Pennsylvania Volunteer Infantry
Credit: G.A.R. Post 139 Collection

Gone But Not Forgotten | *Civil War Veterans of Northeastern Pennsylvania*

Patrick Delacy, Moscow Cemetery
Credit: Ryan Lindbuchler Photo

FREDERICK LYMAN HITCHCOCK
April 18, 1837 – October 11, 1924

On the evening of December 13, 1862, a young lawyer turned soldier lay on the cold field of battle at Fredericksburg among the dead and wounded. Shivering, bleeding, and dazed from the wounds he had suffered, he slowly recovered from the unconsciousness that had seized his body when struck in the head by shell fragment hours before in the heat of battle. The peculiar whine of minié balls filled the air above him and sharply reminded the young adjutant that certain death was just inches away. Frederick Hitchcock had faced death at the Battle of Antietam months before, but had never come so close to it as he had this night. The twenty-five-year-old must have thought back to his former life in Scranton and perhaps longed to be back at his law practice.

Frederick L. Hitchcock was born in Waterbury, Connecticut, to Mr. and Mrs. Daniel Hitchcock, and was educated in public schools there. The Hitchcock family had its foundations with the Puritans and had helped to form the New Haven (Connecticut) colony in the late 1600s. Hitchcock's great-grandfather had served under General Artemus Ward in the American Revolution and had taken part in the battles of Trenton and Brandywine and had been one of the four soldiers to carry the wounded French General Lafayette from the field of battle. Perhaps as a youth, Hitchcock listened to the thrilling tales of his grandfather and wished to experience war for himself.

When Hitchcock was a young man and the family relocated to Scranton, he decided to study law. He studied under Edmund L. Dana of Wilkes-Barre, Pennsylvania. Dana is the subject of another biography in this book. Admitted to the bar of Luzerne County in 1860, Hitchcock began a law practice in Scranton by the age of twenty-three.

In 1862, Hitchcock's practice was interrupted by the events of the Civil War. In June, he received the sad news that his brother, Captain Edwin Hitchcock of the 7th Connecticut Volunteer Infantry, had been killed while leading his men in battle at James Island, South Carolina. Perhaps inspired by his brother's ultimate sacrifice, or wishing for revenge on the southern nation, he looked into joining the 132nd Pennsylvania Volunteer Infantry Regiment, a nine-month regiment that was forming in August of that year. Because of his professional status, he was mustered into service as the regiment's adjutant. An adjutant's duties included various tasks for the regiment's colonel and lieutenant colonel such as performing reconnaissance, doing administrative chores, communicating orders and fulfilling any other duties that the colonel might see fit. The position carried with it the rank of lieutenant and much responsibility.

He had performed these duties well in battle at South Mountain and at Antietam in September of 1862, when the regiment was attached to the II Corps, Army of the Potomac. Lieutenant Hitchcock was still serving as adjutant when the regiment entered the fray at Fredericksburg on December 13, 1862. The Corps was ordered to perform a suicidal frontal assault on a well-fortified Confederate position outside of town at the base of a large hill known as Marye's Heights. The regiment charged valiantly into the face of cold steel and hot lead, and many men of the 132nd fell that day. The book *Advance the Colors!*, describes the following episode during one assault on the heights:

> Lieutenant Charles M. McDougall (Company C) grabbed one of the banners and called to the regimental adjutant, Frederick L. Hitchcock, to help him replace the fallen color-guard so the colors could be kept aloft. As McDougall handed one of the flags to Hitchcock, a bullet crashed into his [McDougall's] arm and wrist, spattering warm blood over Hitchcock's face. Hitchcock took the staff as McDougall fell, only to see another bullet cut the pole in half below his hand. Seconds later, Hitchcock was struck on the head by a shell fragment and fell unconscious. (411-12)

When Hitchcock awoke from unconsciousness, he made a mad rush for the Union line and was wounded in the ankle by an enemy minié ball. He recovered from his wounds and was promoted to the rank of major in January of 1863. He commanded the regiment at the Battle of Chancellorsville in May and was mustered out of service with the rest of the regiment on May 24, 1863. Hitchcock, feeling that he could be of further service to his country, applied to be commissioned an officer in the regular army. In December of 1863, he was awarded the rank of lieutenant colonel of colored troops and immediately set about recruiting the 25th United States Colored Troops in the city of Philadelphia.

The regiment was successfully recruited and sent south to Florida to serve at Fort Pickens. Early in 1864 Hitchcock was promoted to colonel and served as inspector-general of West Florida. During this period, his regiment was noted for its proficiency at drill, complementing Hitchcock's proficiency at command. He returned home in January of 1865 to marry Caroline N. Kingsbury, of Honesdale, Pennsylvania. She was the daughter of a former state senator, Ebenezer Kingsbury. When the war ended in May of 1865, Hitchcock was offered the chance to command the regiment as a part of the regular army. He declined the offer and was mustered out of service on December 6, 1865.

In 1866 upon returning home, Hitchcock became a partner with W.C. Dickinson in a glassware firm, and set up a business on Lackawanna Avenue in Scranton. In future years, he would take on other partners in the business, including future mayor and fellow war veteran, Ezra H. Ripple. In 1875, Hitchcock retired from the business to resume his law practice. Years earlier, he had been instrumental in the formation of Lackawanna County, working in Harrisburg for several months on the law that would create Lackawanna County from a portion of Luzerne County. As a reward, he was appointed to be the county's first prothonotary in 1878. His rigorous "retirement" would next lead him to become a partner in a real estate business (Robertson & Hitchcock). The company was very lucrative and was partially responsible for the paving of several city streets in Scranton in 1882.

Hitchcock's military experience would lead him to be partly responsible for the formation of the Scranton City Guard, in which he again served as adjutant. When the 13th Pennsylvania National Guard was formed in 1878, Hitchcock agreed to serve as the regiment's lieutenant colonel and would later serve as colonel from 1883 to 1888. In 1906 he was appointed city treasurer and served in this capacity until 1909.

His pursuits were not limited to professional and civic duties, but extended to social and religious activities as well. He was very active with the Scranton Presbyterian Church, where he served as a ruling elder and was superintendent of several Presbyterian schools. He was president of the YMCA from 1875 to 1877 and was an active member of the local Masonic lodge. He also served as president of the Lackawanna Historical Society and was the director of the Pennsylvania Oral School for the deaf. Hitchcock wrote several books, including *History of Scranton and its People*, and *War from the Inside, The Story of the 132nd Regiment Pennsylvania Volunteer Infantry in the War for the Suppression of the Rebellion.*

After leading a very active life, Hitchcock passed away in Scranton at the age of eighty-seven in 1924. Along with Ezra Ripple and a few others, Hitchcock was a well-known and honored citizen of the city of Scranton in the 19th and 20th centuries. His legacy of public service, duty, and honor serves as a shining example of patriotism difficult to equal. One may visit his final resting place at the Dunmore Cemetery among many of his comrades who served together as the "boys in blue" during our nation's greatest struggle.

Gone But Not Forgotten | *Civil War Veterans of Northeastern Pennsylvania*

Major Frederick L. Hitchcock, Staff, 132ND Pennsylvania Volunteer Infantry
Credit: G.A.R. Post 139 Collection

Colonel Frederick L. Hitchcock, 13th Pennsylvania National Guard, about 1886
Credit: G.A.R. Post 139 Collection

BENJAMIN FRANKLIN SHARPLESS
May 22, 1841 - October 6, 1922

Benjamin Sharpless was born to a middle class family in Slabtown, Pennsylvania, and grew up around Bloomsburg. Not much is known about his early life except for the fact that he earned his living as a clerk in Bloomsburg. When war broke out, he was nineteen years old and willing to serve his country in her time of need. Like other young men in Bloomsburg, he chose to join Company A of the 6th Pennsylvania Reserves in July of 1861. Along with him that day was a young man by the name of Chester Furman, a future Medal of Honor winner, whose biography is also presented in this book. Company A was known as the "Iron Guards" and would serve the army in some of the bloodiest battles of the Civil War. Its captain was Wellington Ent, who would later become colonel of the regiment and lead it valiantly in battle. Ent is the subject of yet another biography in this book.

The regiment was attached to the newly raised Pennsylvania Reserve Division and was trained during the summer of 1861 in the art of war. While in training camp at Langley, Virginia, Sharpless was stricken with "camp fever" and was quite delirious as a result. He recovered and accompanied the regiment when it was first engaged in battle at Drainesville. Sharpless survived unscathed and was encamped with the regiment over the winter without incident. It was during this time that the 6th Reserves was attached to the V Corps, where it remained during its entire existence. In August, 1862, the regiment was engaged in battle at Second Bull Run and took substantial losses, only to meet the enemy again two weeks later at the Battle of South Mountain.

At the Battle of Antietam on September 17, the regiment repelled an assault by Confederates through the now famous Miller Cornfield. Sharpless and the rest of the regiment were able to repel the Confederate infantry assault, but were fired on by Confederate artillery in mid morning. It was during this artillery barrage that Sharpless was hit in the hip, near the spine, by a large piece of shrapnel. Shrapnel are fragments of metal that scatter when an artillery shell explodes upon impact with the ground, or by a timing fuse within the shell that explodes in mid air, acting as an anti-personnel device. The shrapnel was removed at a nearby field hospital and Sharpless recovered relatively quickly. He had barely survived the bloodiest day of the Civil War.

Sharpless was with the regiment at Fredericksburg in December of 1862 and survived unhurt. In April of 1863 he was promoted to the rank of corporal for his efficient service. In 1863, the regiment took part in the battles of Gettysburg, Bristoe Station, and Mine Run, serving the army

well. In 1864 the Army had a new leader, Ulysses S. Grant, and the men of the 6th Reserves hoped he would see the war through to a successful conclusion. The regiment would take part in Grant's spring campaign of 1864, taking heavy losses. However, Benjamin Sharpless emerged unscathed. He served with the regiment at the battles of the Wilderness, Spotsylvania, North Anna, and Bethesda Church. Its term of service was up soon after, and the regiment was mustered out at Harrisburg on June 13, 1864.

Sharpless returned home to Bloomsburg with the remainder of the Iron Guards to a large celebration held in their honor. Sharpless was married a year later on December 26, 1865 to Sophia Hartman of Bloomsburg. The young couple had their first child, Edward, in 1866 and a second child, Frank, in 1868. Sadly, both boys died in 1870 of unknown causes. The couple would have four more sons (Joseph – 1871, Charles – 1873, Raymond – 1877, and Arthur – 1879) who would live to adulthood.

The couple would lead a good life in Bloomsburg for the next fifty-one years while he worked as a clerk. In 1914, Sophia died, leaving Sharpless alone. According to pension records, he received $30 per month in 1916 as compensation for his disability due to "rheumatism, right wrist pain [apparently, it was broken and dislocated during his service], heart disease, back and side pain from his wound, and piles." By the time of his death in 1922, he was receiving $50 per month.

Benjamin Franklin Sharpless died at the family home on Centre Street in Bloomsburg of heart disease on October 6, 1922. He was eighty-one years of age. His remains were laid to rest at the Rosemont Cemetery in Bloomsburg next to his wife Sophia. In the same cemetery, lie the remains of his colonel, Wellington Ent, and his friend, Chester Furman, all heroes of the "Iron Guards."

Gone But Not Forgotten | *Civil War Veterans of Northeastern Pennsylvania*

CORPORAL BENJAMIN F. SHARPLESS, CO. A, 6TH PENNSYLVANIA RESERVES
CREDIT: CATHERINE VANDERSLICE COLLECTION

CHARLES C. BETTERLY
April 14, 1838 – May 1, 1921

An interesting article on Charles C. Betterly of the 143rd Pennsylvania Volunteer Infantry Regiment appeared in the *Wilkes-Barre Record* on May 2, 1921. His story is truly an exciting and compelling one. His military and pension records, along with this article, tell the story of a man with unique experiences.

Charles Betterly was born in Berwick, Pennsylvania, on a spring day in 1838. His father, William, was a carpenter by trade and taught his son this trade. At the age of fifteen, Betterly moved to Wilkes-Barre, Pennsylvania, with his family and continued to work with his father as a carpenter. During this time, he also joined a local fire company as a volunteer fire fighter. When war broke out in 1861, Betterly had just turned twenty-three years of age. Unlike many other young men, he decided not to volunteer for military service right away. Perhaps his parents convinced him to wait and see what would happen as the war progressed.

By the following summer, it was painfully obvious that the war would not be over soon, and recruitment of Pennsylvania regiments continued in the Commonwealth. One such regiment was recruited almost exclusively in Luzerne County and was called the 143rd Pennsylvania Infantry Regiment. Many local men flocked to the training camp at Luzerne, Pennsylvania, and enlisted in the service for a period of three years. One of those men was Betterly, who enlisted in Company C. He enlisted on August 4, 1862, at Luzerne and was described as being 5'7" tall, having a fair complexion, blue eyes, and light hair. His brother, Edward, enlisted in the 165th New York Infantry Regiment soon after. During the course of the war Edward would become assistant surgeon of that regiment.

At Camp Luzerne, the regiment spent the next two months drilling and learning to become soldiers. In November, the 143rd regiment was sent south to Harrisburg, then to Washington, where it was sent to the front to join the famous "bucktail brigade" consisting of the 149th and 150th Pennsylvania Infantry Regiments. The brigade spent the winter drilling and was attached to the I Corps, Army of the Potomac. In May of 1863, Betterly fought with his regiment at Chancellorsville where the Union army was soundly defeated by Confederate forces. The 143rd sustained light casualties but would lose many at the Battle of Gettysburg two months later.

The I Corps reached the field at Gettysburg just in time to slow down the Confederate army, which was pushing towards the heights beyond Gettysburg. These heights, called Cemetery Hill and Cemetery Ridge, were strong positions that could become impregnable if defended

properly. It was the task of the Corps, along with the 143rd regiment, to slow down the invading Confederate forces long enough to allow the rest of the Union army to occupy those heights. On that day, July 1, 1863, many men of the 143rd would fall in battle. The regiment took heavy casualties and was eventually pushed through the town and to the heights, but had succeeded in allowing time for the Union army to occupy Cemetery Ridge. Betterly took part in the action and was disabled when a right inguinal hernia erupted. He was doubled over with pain and spent the remainder of the battle at a field hospital behind the Union line.

On July 4, he was sent to a hospital at Baltimore, Maryland, to recover from his ailment. After his recovery, he was sent on detached duty. While on this duty, he helped round up deserters (men who had run away from their regiments without leave) and took part in a skirmish with Confederate guerrillas under Colonel John S. Mosby. He was sent back to the regiment that fall, but was disabled with a bad case of diarrhea and was sent to a hospital at Philadelphia until March of 1864. In May, the regiment was heavily engaged at the Battle of the Wilderness and lost almost half of its 450-men. Betterly was among the wounded that day. The nature of the wound is unknown to the author, but it was serious enough to result in his hospitalization at Philadelphia once again.

In August of 1864, Betterly was given a furlough. He returned home to Wilkes-Barre to his parents for a period of almost three months. He returned to the 143rd by the winter of 1864-65, but was again detached for special service in March of 1865. The following month, Betterly was in Washington on this detached service and decided to see a play, perhaps for his birthday. The play was entitled "Our American Cousin" and was being performed at Ford's Theater. On the evening of April 14, 1865, Betterly put on his uniform and went to the theater. It was there that he witnessed the assassination of President Abraham Lincoln by John Wilkes Booth.

Betterly took part in a search for the assassin, being assigned to a search party. After Booth was killed by Union troops in late April, Betterly was assigned to act as a body guard at the funeral of President Lincoln. He performed this service well and returned to his regiment at Hart's Island, New York, where it was guarding prisoners and escorting new recruits to the front. He was mustered out with his company on June 12, 1865, and returned home to Wilkes-Barre.

Betterly returned to the life of a carpenter and married Medora A. Bowman at Carverton on September 17, 1872. The couple began a family, and Medora gave birth to eight children during the course of their marriage. Austin was born in 1874, C. Bow in 1875, Susan in 1876, Edward in 1879, William in 1881, Ithel in 1886, Olen in 1888, and Mary in 1890. In 1873, Betterly moved to Pottsville, Pennsylvania. It was during this time that he served on a jury that convicted members of the famed "Molly Maguires." The family returned to Wilkes-Barre in 1876, moving to North Main Street, where Betterly started a lucrative business in the awning manufacturing industry.

Betterly did very well in the industry and was able to provide a good life for his family. After his retirement, he received a government pension amounting to $15 per month in 1912, and $30 in 1921. Because he had witnessed such an important event in United States history, he was looked upon as somewhat of a celebrity by the people of the city of Wilkes-Barre, and enjoyed much notoriety. He passed away at his home in 1921 and was interred in the Hollenback Cemetery, where he was given a government stone that plainly reads "C.C. Betterly, Co. C, 143rd PA INF." Medora Betterly joined her husband in eternal rest in 1925.

PRIVATE CHARLES C. BETTERLY, CO. C, 143RD PENNSYLVANIA VOLUNTEER INFANTRY
CREDIT: REPRINTED WITH PERMISSION OF THE TIMES LEADER NEWSPAPER

CHESTER S. FURMAN
February 14, 1842 – July 22, 1912

During the long hot days of the summer of 1861, northeast Pennsylvania, as well as most of the North, was stricken with war fever. Just four months earlier the opening shots of the Civil War were fired at Fort Sumter, South Carolina. The newly elected president, Abraham Lincoln, called for the loyal states in the North to mobilize hundreds of thousands of troops. Many young men, feeling the war would be over quickly and not wanting to miss the excitement, rushed to enlist in the Army. On July 13, a company was being raised in Bloomsburg, Pennsylvania, called the "Iron Guards," and was to serve with the 6th Pennsylvania Reserve Infantry.

A young harness maker from town enthusiastically rushed to serve the Union. When he enlisted, Chester Furman was described as twenty years of age, 5'9" in height, having blue eyes and a light complexion. This young man was born in Columbia County and had lived near or in Bloomsburg all of his life. All he had known was northeastern Pennsylvania, and now he saw his chance to see the nation and be a part of history in the making. Furman had joined up with most of his friends from town, like Benjamin Sharpless, the subject of another biography in this book. One can reflect on the feeling of security that exists when friends set out to accomplish a great task as a group.

The 6th Reserves was attached to the Reserve Division of Pennsylvania and would see some of the hardest fighting of the war. The regiment was taught how to march, live, and fight like soldiers in the summer and fall of 1861, and spent the winter in camp rather uneventfully. It was attached to the V Corps and remained at this assignment for the rest of its service and was first engaged in battle in August of 1862 at Second Bull Run. Unfortunately, it was a Union defeat and the army was forced from the field. Two weeks later, the regiment would again meet the enemy at South Mountain in an attempt to prevent Robert E. Lee's Confederate Army from invading the North. It proved to be a skirmish when compared to the Battle of Antietam on September 17, 1862. The regiment repelled a Confederate infantry attack through the Miller Cornfield and sustained considerable casualties, one of them being Chester's friend Benjamin Sharpless, who had been wounded by artillery fire that day. The battle was a success, and the Confederate invasion of the north was stopped…for now.

The 6th Reserves would next meet the enemy at Fredericksburg, Virginia, on December 13, 1862. In this disastrous battle, the regiment would lose 119 men out of 375 who went into battle. Furman survived unhurt but frustrated, like most other Federal soldiers, at the incompetence of

his commanding generals. The regiment spent the remainder of the winter in camp, resting and recuperating from the losses it had sustained. When the regiment left for war a year earlier, it had about one thousand men, now it numbered only about 250. Furman was promoted to the rank of corporal on April 15, 1863, for his bravery and experience.

The spring of 1863 brought new hope to the army as the new commanding general, Joseph Hooker, promised a great victory for the North. The Battle of Chancellorsville in May resulted in perhaps the largest tactical blunder of the war, and the Union army was soundly defeated once again in the countryside of Virginia. The 6th did not participate in this battle, but it would not be long until it would meet the enemy in July of 1863. The Battle of Gettysburg had been under way for one day when the 6th Reserves reached the field on July 2. As part of the Fifth Corps, the 6th fought the enemy near Little Round Top, trying desperately to repel the furious Confederate attack on the position. The men of the brigade were receiving deadly sniper fire from a log house located nearby. The colonel asked for volunteers to assault and drive the Confederates from the house. When the request was made, six brave men immediately stepped forward. One of those was Chester Furman. At great risk, the six men slowly made their way under a tremendous fire. When they were within close distance, they made a mad dash for the door, broke it down with the butts of their muskets, and demanded the surrender of the twenty Confederates within, which included one officer and several Federal prisoners. The position was captured, saving the lives of countless numbers of Federal troops near Little Round Top and Devil's Den.

Following the great Union victory at Gettysburg, the regiment fought at Bristoe Station and Mine Run. Again, Furman survived each battle unhurt, and volunteered for service with the U.S. Signal Corps in October of 1863. The Signal Corps employed about 1,500 men, and its main mission was to serve the Federal Army, providing communication between commands by using flags, telegraph lines, pistols, rockets, and torches. It would receive and pass on messages between commands regarding Federal positions as well as Confederate positions in the field, and was a valuable service to the Federal Army. Chester served in the Corps for the next nine months and was mustered out of the Army at City Point, Virginia, on July 13, 1864. In the photograph provided, one can see the insignia of the Signal Corps (crossed signal flags) attached to Furman's hat. He had survived the bloodiest years of the war without being wounded or captured.

Furman returned to Bloomsburg a hero, and once again saw his friend Ben Sharpless, who also had survived the war. He resumed his trade as a harness maker and was married in November of 1868 to a local woman named Sarah. Together the couple had six children: Josiah, Julia, Harvey, Boyd, Chester, and Clara. They lived a long life together, and in 1893 Furman was receiving a government pension of $8 per month for the reason of rheumatism and heart disease as a result of his service in the war. In August of 1897, Chester received word that Congress had awarded him the Congressional Medal of Honor for his heroic actions at Gettysburg. Recognition for his actions must have been a great compliment for Furman.

On July 22, 1912, the great hero died at his home in Bloomsburg at the age of seventy. He was laid to rest at the Rosemont Cemetery in Bloomsburg, not too far from Ben Sharpless and the colonel of the 6th Reserves, Wellington Ent. Four years later, Sarah would join Furman in eternal rest at Rosemont.

Gone But Not Forgotten | *Civil War Veterans of Northeastern Pennsylvania*

CORPORAL CHESTER FURMAN, CO. A, 6TH PENNSYLVANIA RESERVES
CREDIT: WILLIAM ELSWICK COLLECTION

Edmund Lovell Dana
January 29, 1817 – April 25, 1889

The Dana family has a long and prestigious history in the Wyoming Valley. The first member of the family settled in New England about 1640, and descendants were among the first to settle in the Valley. Anderson Dana, Edmund's grandfather, practiced law in Pittston and Wilkes-Barre until his murder by pro-British Native Americans at the Battle of Wyoming in July of 1778. Anderson's son Asa would marry Ann Pruner, the daughter of a prominent Hanover Township judge. They would give birth to their first child, Edmund, in 1817.

Born in Wilkes-Barre, Edmund Dana would spend most of his early life on his father's farm near the town of Eaton, near Tunkhannock, Pennsylvania. In 1832, at the age of fifteen, Dana entered the old Wilkes-Barre Academy, and entered Yale University (then College) in 1835 as a sophomore. After graduation in 1838, Dana worked as a civil engineer on the North Branch Canal, which extended from the Northeastern Pennsylvania to New York State.

Dana studied law under a prominent judge in Wilkes Barre and gained admittance to the bar of Luzerne County in 1841. Always having an interest in military affairs, Dana enthusiastically joined the newly formed local company of state militia, called the "Wyoming Artillerists" the following year, and was commissioned first lieutenant and then captain of the company. Also in 1842, Dana married Sarah Peters, of Philadelphia. They would later have a son named Charles.

In 1846 the United States government declared war on Mexico and issued a call for troops. Captain Dana's company was one of the first to embark and was designated Company I, 1st Regiment, Pennsylvania Volunteers. The regiment served heroically for the next two years and was engaged in several battles. At the battle of Cerro Gordo in 1847, the company, under Dana's command, captured large numbers of Mexican prisoners. Dana received special mention by General Winfield Scott's staff for bravery and good command at the siege of Pueblo and for leading a charge at El Pinal Pass. At the close of war in 1848, Dana's company was mustered out of Federal service and was welcomed home to the Wyoming Valley with much enthusiasm.

He returned to his law practice, but never deserted his military interests. He was commissioned major general of the 9th Division of the state militia in the ten years leading up to the outbreak of the Civil War. He ran for Congress in 1851 and for state senator in 1853, but was defeated each time.

In 1862, with the Civil War raging for a year, Dana was appointed commandant of Camp Luzerne. Camp Luzerne was based on the farmland in and around the modern-day Borough

of Luzerne and served as a training ground for a newly formed regiment, almost exclusively made up of men recruited from Luzerne County, called the 143rd Pennsylvania Volunteer Infantry Regiment. Dana was elected colonel in October of that year and the regiment set off for the front where it was attached to the I Corps under General John F. Reynolds, another Pennsylvania native.

The regiment was engaged in the Battle of Chancellorsville in May of 1863 and suffered many casualties. But Gettysburg would be the ultimate test for Dana and his regiment of Luzerne County natives. The regiment, attached to the now famous bucktail brigade, was one of the first to reach the field at Gettysburg. Vastly outnumbered by charging Confederate divisions, the regiment was badly decimated, and the brigade commander fell mortally wounded. Dana took command of the brigade and led it in a somewhat orderly retreat to Cemetery Ridge. He was described as cool and calm by his men and looked upon as a hero and an inspiration.

At the Battle of the Wilderness on May 5, 1864, Colonel Dana was wounded by an enemy musket ball and taken prisoner by Confederate forces. He was imprisoned at Macon, Georgia, and then Charleston, South Carolina, enduring much hardship and deprivation. Thankfully, he was given food and protection by a Confederate major named Raymond who had been a classmate of Dana's at Yale. During his imprisonment at Charleston, Confederates placed him and some fifty other prisoners under Federal naval fire as retaliation for some breach of the rules of war by the Federal Government. Dana survived this harrowing experience and was exchanged as a prisoner in August of 1864. He returned to his regiment and immediately took command in time for the siege of Petersburg, Virginia.

The regiment performed honorably at Petersburg and operations thereafter, but was assigned to special duty North in February of 1865 because of its greatly reduced numbers due to casualties. It performed guard duty at Hart's Island, New York City harbor, where it escorted recruits and convalescents to the front. The regiment was mustered out on June 12, 1865 with the exception of Dana. He served on court-martial duty until August of that year and was brevetted brigadier-general for his service before he was mustered out on June 23.

Following the war, Dana resumed his law practice and defeated Henry M. Hoyt in 1867 to become judge of Luzerne County. He served for ten years in this position and retired in 1878 at the age of sixty-one.

In his retirement, Dana involved himself in various positions that seem to have left little time for relaxation. He served as president of the Wilkes-Barre City Council; director of the First National Bank; vice president of the Wyoming Memorial Association; president of the Osterhout Free Library; president of the Society of the Army of the Potomac; member of Masonic Lodge 61 of Wilkes-Barre; and charter member and first president of the Wyoming Historical and Geological Society (currently the Luzerne County Historical Society). He spoke at various functions and was looked upon as a great friend by the people of northeastern Pennsylvania.

In 1888 he suffered a stroke and lost the ability to speak, and his strength and memory were also affected. Finally, on Thursday, April 25, 1889 he succumbed to his affliction and died at his home on South Main Street in Wilkes-Barre. He was interred at the Hollenback Cemetery in Wilkes-Barre where his remains lie today. Edmund L. Dana led a life of public service, ever vigilant to the Union and to the people of the Wyoming Valley. He can truly be looked upon as one of the heroes of our nation and the Commonwealth of Pennsylvania.

Colonel Edmund L. Dana, Staff, 143rd Pennsylvania Volunteer Infantry
Credit: Roger D. Hunt Collection

ELI E. CORWIN
1833 – April 3, 1906

The brief military career of a carpenter-turned-soldier began on September 15, 1862, at Montrose, Pennsylvania. Eli Corwin was described as being 5'7" in height, having a fair complexion, blue eyes, and light hair. He was born in Susquehanna County and lived in New Milford, Pennsylvania. The war had been going for over a year when he enlisted in Company B of the 17th Pennsylvania Volunteer Cavalry, made up of men from across the Commonwealth. His enlistment was for three years and he received a $25 bounty as an incentive for his service.

The regiment was organized at Camp Simmons in Harrisburg, and was trained in the skills of cavalrymen in the fall of 1862. It was issued sabers, pistols, and most importantly, horses. Once its training was completed in November, the regiment was sent to Washington, and thence to the front. There it was engaged at Occoquan by Confederate cavalry under Wade Hampton. The 17th performed admirably, along with the 2nd Pennsylvania Cavalry, in foiling many attempts by the enemy to cross the river. Private Corwin took part in the action but was hindered by a severe hernia that had been brought on by the horse riding that goes along with life in a cavalry regiment.

The regiment returned to Stafford Court House in January of 1863, and Corwin was examined by the regimental surgeon and sent to a nearby field hospital for treatment. The Army surgeons found him unfit for further service and he was discharged on January 27. Corwin returned home and resumed his life as a carpenter. He received an army pension for his injury that amounted to $12 per month in 1903. He moved to Williams Street in Scranton sometime in the late 19th century and remained a bachelor by all indications. By 1900, his physician had stated that physical labor was impossible for Corwin due to his hernia, rheumatism, and heart disease. He died in the spring of 1906 and was buried at the Forrest Hill Cemetery in Scranton.

Private Eli E. Corwin, Co. B, 17th Pennsylvania Volunteer Cavalry
Credit: G.A.R. Post 139 Collection

GEORGE SCHLAGER
January 20, 1843 – March 25, 1911

The "Bethlehem Cavalry" was recruited in the summer of 1861, just as the people of the North and South were preparing for a long, bloody war. The Bethlehem Cavalry would be made up of men from Northampton County and would serve as Company A of the 4th Pennsylvania Cavalry Regiment. On August 7, 1861, an eighteen-year-old marble polisher / confectioner from Bethlehem would take an oath to serve the Union cause. His name was George Schlager. Born in Green County, New York, Schlager had moved to Bethlehem, Pennsylvania, some years earlier. According to company records, he was described as being 5'5" in height, having brown eyes, light hair, and a light complexion.

The regiment was transported south to Harrisburg, then to Washington, where it spent the winter training and preparing for the upcoming spring campaigns of 1862. After it was furnished with horses and appropriate weapons, the regiment took the field under Major General Irvin McDowell's command in May of 1862. It performed admirably and was transferred to the Army of the Potomac in June of 1862 in order to take part in the Peninsula Campaign. It took part in several battles during the campaign including Mechanicsville, Gaines' Mill, and Malvern Hill. At Antietam on September 17, 1862, the regiment supported an artillery battery where the brigade commander and former regimental commander, Colonel James H. Childs, was disemboweled by an enemy cannonball.

During the winter of 1862-63 the regiment took part in several skirmishes throughout northern Virginia, taking relatively light casualties. Schlager remained with the company, performing his duties with skill and dedication. In March of 1863, the 4th regiment took part in a fight against Confederate cavalry at Kelly's Ford and was successful in defeating the enemy. During the Chancellorsville campaign, the regiment, along with the rest of the Cavalry Corps, took part in an unsuccessful raid behind Confederate lines.

During the Gettysburg campaign, the 4th was engaged at the Battle of Brandy Station on June 9, where it put up a good fight against Confederate cavalry under General J.E.B. Stuart. Also, it was engaged in skirmishing at Aldie, Upperville, and Middleburg, reaching the Army of the Potomac on July 2, 1863. There, the 4th served as guard to General Alfred Pleasanton, then commander of the Cavalry Corps. On the afternoon of July 3, the regiment came under Confederate artillery fire, but sustained few losses.

On October 12, 1863, the 4th was given orders to support the 13th Pennsylvania Cavalry at

Jeffersonville, Virginia. The 13th had been driven from the town by a Confederate force earlier that day and awaited the support of the 4th to retake the town. The regiments attacked and drove the enemy from the town, but were later attacked by a large Confederate force. The two regiments were surrounded, cut off, and largely captured. The 4th regiment had gone into battle with about 375 men and lost approximately two hundred in the battle. Most of those captured would be sent south to Andersonville prison in Georgia, where many would succumb to weakness and starvation at the hands of their captors. Schlager was fortunate enough to be one of those men who escaped capture.

Because of the decimation of the regiment, the remaining men of the 4th regiment were ordered to act as guards for the Orange and Alexandria Railroad through the winter of 1863-64. There, the men performed scouting duties, ridding the countryside of Confederate guerrillas. In January of 1864, the term of enlistment for the men of the regiment was up, but two thirds of the men decided to re-enlist, assuring that the regimental organization would remain intact. Schlager re-enlisted on January 1, 1864, and went home on furlough to Bethlehem with the other "veteran volunteers" in February.

During the remainder of the winter, the regiment's ranks were filled with recruits. It was up to the veterans to teach them how to be good horse soldiers. By spring, the new recruits had been trained, and discipline was well ingrained in the men. The regiment took part in the Battle of the Wilderness, being dispatched from point to point to fill in gaps in the Federal battleline and protect the flanks of the army.

The remainder of the month of May would bring many battles for Schlager and the rest of the 4th cavalry. It was ordered to take part in a raid on the Confederate capital at Richmond where it engaged the enemy at Yellow Tavern, repelling a Confederate charge. It was also engaged at Haw's Shop on May 28, and Cold Harbor in June of 1864, taking heavy losses in all engagements.

At the Battle of Trevilian Station on June 12, the 4th regiment was heavily engaged with the enemy in a desperate fight. The regiment was ordered to capture a railroad that was protected by Confederate cavalry and mounted infantry. Through the desperate fighting, many men fell wounded and killed, but the objective was accomplished, and the enemy fell back in confusion. One of the wounded that day was Private George Schlager. During the fight, a Confederate minié ball was fired into the left side of Schlager's chest, passing through his abdomen and resting in his back, near the base of his spine. Schlager was removed from the field and sent north to Finley Hospital in Washington, then to Chestnut Hill Hospital in Philadelphia. The doctors, while examining his wound, decided that the risk of removing the bullet was greater than the risk of leaving it where it was, and the ball was never removed.

Schlager had returned to his regiment by September and was promoted to the rank of corporal. By this time, the Union army was involved in surrounding and besieging the city of Petersburg, south of Richmond. There the regiment took part in several attempts to cut off Confederate lines of supply by raiding and destroying several railroads, bridges, and outposts. In performing these duties, the 4th cavalry was engaged in several skirmishes/battles with the enemy such as those at Poplar Springs Church and Boydton Plank Road, where it lost several men. On December 1, 1864, the regiment captured two hundred prisoners, three cannon and other important supplies that were being guarded.

While building winter quarters for the regiment's horses later that month, Schlager was wounded when a comrade accidentally struck him in the left heel with an ax. He was sent

to City Point, Virginia, and hospitalized for his wound until February of 1865, when he once again returned to his regiment. In March, Schlager fought with the regiment at Dinwiddie Court House, where many officers and enlisted men were killed and wounded. The last fight that the 4th took part in was at Five Forks, Virginia, where it captured many Confederate troops who were footsore and starving.

Following the surrender of the Confederate army, the regiment was sent to Lynchburg where it performed provost duty, and was mustered out of service on July 1, 1865. Schlager returned to Bethlehem and soon after moved to Scranton. There he met a local woman named Elizabeth Galagher, and the couple was married on June 14, 1868, at St. Peter's Church in Scranton. The couple had four children over the course of their marriage.

Schlager, in much pain from the bullet still lodged in his back, applied to the government for a pension and was receiving $8 per month in 1886, the stipend increasing to $12 per month by the time of his death in 1911. Due to the pain of his wounds, Schlager could not return to his profession of marble polisher, but became a teamster.

The couple lived on Irving Avenue in Scranton until his death on March 25, 1911. Schlager was laid to rest in the Forrest Hill Cemetery in Scranton, his body still carrying the Confederate bullet lodged in it at the battle of Trevilian Station, forty-seven years earlier. His wife Elizabeth joined her husband in death on July 20, 1915.

Corporal George Schlager, Co. A, 4th Pennsylvania Volunteer Cavalry
Credit: G.A.R. Post 139 Collection

GEORGE W. ENGLE
January 11, 1840 – January 15, 1921

If one were to look on the muster rolls of the 143rd Pennsylvania Volunteer Infantry Regiment, one would find the name of George Engle of Company C. At the time of his enlistment on August 4, 1862, he was twenty-one years old, 5'7", had a fair complexion, gray eyes, dark hair, and was born at Easton, Pennsylvania. Engle had lived in Kingston Township, in the modern-day area of the Borough of Luzerne, Pennsylvania, when he enlisted for three years in the 143rd. The regiment, made up almost entirely of men from Luzerne County, was being recruited by a prominent local lawyer, Edmund L. Dana, the subject of another biography in this book.

At the time of his enlistment, Engle, a carpenter by trade, perhaps could not resist the call to arms since the training camp of the regiment was at "Camp Luzerne," a brief walk from his home on Main Street. Upon his enlistment, he received a $25 bonus and was mustered into the regiment on August 27, 1862. The regiment trained in Luzerne until November, when it proceeded to Harrisburg where it was issued Enfield rifled muskets, imported from Great Britain. By the end of the month, the regiment found itself near Washington, at Fort Slocum. It remained there for three months, training and preparing for the upcoming spring campaign. In February it was attached to the third division of the I Corps, Army of the Potomac.

The regiment first met the enemy in battle at Chancellorsville in May of 1863 and sustained light casualties. Perhaps the greatest test for the regiment was at Gettysburg on July 1, 1863. The I Corps was the first infantry corps to reach the field northwest of Gettysburg on that day, and had the daunting task of holding off a tenacious Confederate onslaught. The enemy outnumbered the Union troops by a very large margin, but the officers of the I Corps knew that they had to delay the Confederate rush as long as possible. This delay was needed so the rest of the Army of the Potomac could gather together on the heights south of Gettysburg to face the enemy as one.

General John F. Reynolds, another Pennsylvanian, commanded the I Corps and made a valiant stand against the oncoming Confederate force. As more and more Confederate troops assaulted the Federal position at McPherson's Ridge, the outnumbered Federals began to give way, and a somewhat unorganized retreat began through the town of Gettysburg. The 143rd lost many men in the fighting as they stubbornly resisted while being forced to give ground to Confederate troops. Color Sergeant Benjamin Crippen of Company E, who held the regiment's colors, turned toward the enemy and defiantly shook his fist in anger. He was almost immediately shot down where he stood. Today, one can visit Luzerne and observe the monument dedicated to the 143rd that

includes a likeness of Crippen. Alongside Engle that day was Sergeant James Rutter, who would be awarded the Medal of Honor for saving the life of an officer of Company C.

During this retreat a bullet struck Engle in the back, violently knocking him to the ground. Carried back by his comrades to the newly formed Federal line at Cemetery Ridge, south of Gettysburg, he was immediately sent to a nearby field hospital, where his wounds were treated. The Confederate musketball, lodged in his left scapula, was immediately removed, and Engle was sent to the Cotton Factory General Hospital in Harrisburg in the days following the battle. He was hospitalized there from July to October of 1863, then sent to a hospital at York, Pennsylvania, until March of 1864.

On March 26, 1864, Engle was transferred to the Veteran Reserve Corps. The V.R.C., or "Invalid Corps," was a portion of the Federal army whose men served behind the front lines in various capacities such as prison guards, garrison troops surrounding Washington D.C., assistants at hospitals, and clerks. The purpose of the Veteran Reserve Corps was to free able-bodied men to serve at the front. Engle served with Company 109, 2nd Battalion, at Pittsburgh, Pennsylvania, until he was mustered out of service on July 3, 1865.

After the war, Engle returned to Luzerne and began a business as a merchant. Records suggest he gave up carpentry, but do not indicate what type of merchant he became. He was married to Lydia G. Pettebone at Forty Fort, Pennsylvania, on November 11, 1872. The couple had three children: Arthur – 1875, Bessie – 1876, and Bertha – 1879. Records show that Engle was receiving a pension of $24 per month in 1912, because of the pain he was suffering as a result of the gunshot wound to the back. In 1908 Lydia died, leaving Engle with his three children, who were of course adults at the time. The old veteran died at his Main Street home in Luzerne on January 15, 1921, four days after his eighty-first birthday. He was buried in the Forty Fort Cemetery next to Lydia. It is a stroke of luck that his burial place has remained intact after the Agnes Flood of 1972 devastated the cemetery, washing away many stones and remains.

Gone But Not Forgotten | *Civil War Veterans of Northeastern Pennsylvania*

Private George W. Engle, Co. A, 143rd Pennsylvania Volunteer Infantry
Credit: Sandra Hart Collection

HENRY KRIGBAUM
June 18, 1836 – August 20, 1913

In May of 1863, a tall, lean man lay on a bed in a U.S. Army hospital in Harrisburg, Pennsylvania. Perhaps he thought about his home in Scranton and how he longed to be there. Less than a year earlier, Henry Krigbaum had been in Scranton, Pennsylvania, until duty called. On August 9, 1862, Krigbaum enlisted in the 132nd Pennsylvania Volunteer Infantry for nine months. Perhaps he thought that a three-year enlistment was too long, but nine months just enough time to get a taste of army life and the glory of war. Now, he lay in a hospital, nursing a wound he had suffered at the Battle of Fredericksburg the previous December.

After enlisting in the "Railroad Guards" (Company I), Krigbaum collected a $25 bounty and left Scranton with the regiment for Washington. The regiment trained near the city and was attached to the II Corps, Army of the Potomac, before it took the field. The green regiment was heavily engaged at the battle of Antietam on September 17, charging the "Sunken Lane" portion of the battlefield and losing many men in the fight. Krigbaum got his taste of war, but it was not glorious in any way. The colonel of the regiment, Richard Oakford, was killed in the assault, along with thirty men of the 132nd regiment. The men Krigbaum fought beside were his childhood friends, and he could only do his duty in the fight, hoping that he and his friends would not become the victims of an enemy musket ball. Six men of Krigbaum's company would die that day, and two would be wounded. Krigbaum survived unhurt, but shaken by the deadly art of war.

In October, Krigbaum was detached to serve as a cook in the II Corps field hospital, and served in this capacity until December. On December 13, 1862, the II Corps was given the order to carry out a frontal assault on the Confederate position outside of Fredericksburg, Virginia. The newly-appointed commander of the Army of the Potomac, Major General Ambrose Burnside, was more than ready to punish the Confederate Army there. Unfortunately, his plan of attack degenerated into a massive assault by Union forces against an impenetrable position on a hill known as "Marye's Heights." The 132nd carried out its orders and assaulted the hill, losing 150 of 340 men. According to Bates' *History of Pennsylvania Volunteers*:

> An incident which occurred in this battle well illustrates the valor and determination which fired the hearts of the citizen soldiery in this war.

John Kistler, a private of Company F, had his arm blown off at the elbow by a cannon ball, as the regiment entered the fight. With his arm bandaged, he still kept the field, and as the shattered ranks came back from the bloody assault, he rushed up to the Colonel, saying, 'We shall whip them yet'. (Volume VII, 244)

Kistler was later buried in the Mauch Chunk Cemetery in Jim Thorpe upon his death in 1916. Krigbaum was also wounded in the arm that day. The surgeon of the 132nd regiment stated that his arm was wounded "severely." Even though it was injured in this manner, it was not amputated, as was the case with most grievous wounds of the period. Krigbaum was sent to the hospital at Harrisburg to recover and remained there until his discharge on May 24, 1863. Krigbaum returned to Scranton where he died fifty years later. He was buried in the Forrest Hill Cemetery in Scranton, where he remains today.

Private Henry L. Krigbaum, Co. I, 132ⁿᵈ Pennsylvania Volunteer Infantry
Credit: G.A.R. Post 139 Collection

Hiram W. Pursell
August 1, 1837 – May 13, 1918

A twenty-four-year old boatman by the name of Hiram Pursell was mustered into the newly recruited 104th Pennsylvania Volunteer Infantry Regiment at Doylestown, Pennsylvania, on September 16, 1861. The state of Pennsylvania was responding to the call for troops by the recently elected President Abraham Lincoln. The regiment's recruits were entirely from Bucks County, and led by Colonel William Davis, a prominent citizen, Mexican War veteran and former colonel of the 25th Pennsylvania Volunteer Infantry Regiment (a ninety-day regiment). The men of the company elected Pursell to the rank of corporal before the regiment left for Washington, D.C., on November 6. On the muster rolls, he is listed as being 6' tall (tall for that era), having a dark complexion, dark eyes, and black hair.

The regiment was trained at Washington and was attached to the IV Corps. It took the field the following spring under the command of General George B. McClellan and first met the enemy at Yorktown and Savage's Station, where it performed admirably as a new regiment. The regiment's greatest test would occur at the Battle of Fair Oaks on May 31, 1862. The regiment was ordered to defend a battery of artillery (four guns) and was posted along a road. Confederates soon appeared at the front, their numbers increasing by the minute. A charge was ordered, and the men fixed bayonets and sprang forward with a yell toward the oncoming Confederates. The men advanced about one hundred yards and crossed over a rail fence. Waiting for reinforcements, the regiment held its ground and kept up a withering fire upon the enemy. However, when reinforcements never arrived, the enemy began to outnumber the 104th regiment and forced them to withdrawal. Pursell was acting color sergeant at this time and held the national colors out in front of the men, past the rail fence. He had been ordered to move to the rear with the flag when he noticed that the other flag (the regimental flag) was left standing alone, with the staff stuck in the ground. According to the book *Deeds of Valor*, the following drama ensued:

> Color-Sergeant Pursell had already secured his own standard, and, with it in his hands, he jumped over the fence and seized the other. The enemy saw the movement, and five of their men rushed forward at the same time, still keeping up their fire. Pursell reached it first, seized the staff, and sprang for the fence with both flags in his hands. As he mounted the fence he was struck by a bullet in the left thigh and fell, carrying the colors with

him. Getting to his feet again he ran about 500 yards, handed one flag to Sergeant Myers, and started for the rear with the other, but, becoming faint from the loss of blood, he gave it to Corporal Mitchner and fell exhausted on the field, having received two slight wounds in the arm and neck. He was rescued by General Casey's bugler, Israel Stidinger, who took him on his horse to Savage Station. The flags were brought off the field in safety and delivered to the regiment after the battle. (42)

An artist's rendition of this event, painted in 1899 by William Trego, appears on the cover of the volume that you are presently reading.

During the period of the Civil War, the colors of each regiment were highly respected by the men. It was considered dishonorable to lose one's colors to the enemy, and very heroic to capture an enemy's colors. Only the best enlisted men in the regiment were allowed to carry the colors, a deadly assignment because the enemy would always want to dishearten a regiment by killing or wounding its flag bearer, and possibly capturing the colors. Even though the fatality rate for color bearers was very high, it was considered the most honorable and valuable position in the regiment. Colors also served a practical purpose in that they enabled the men to keep track of their regiment's position in a battle filled with confusion, black powder smoke and deadly enemy fire. If the colors went forward, the regiment followed. The reverse was also true. By saving the colors that day, Pursell showed great courage.

The regiment was transferred south to aid in the capture of Confederate coastal fortifications in the Carolinas. After recovering, Pursell rejoined the regiment to take part in the siege of Charleston, South Carolina, and the siege of the now famous Fort Wagner along the South Carolina coast in 1863. The regiment served bravely and accomplished most of what it had been asked to do.

On September 30, 1864, most of Company G, including Pursell, was mustered out of service because the term of enlistment had expired. The regiment continued, however, because several hundred draftees and volunteers had been mustered into the ranks of the 104th. Not much is known about the life of Pursell after the Civil War. What is known is that in 1894 he was awarded the nation's highest decoration: the Medal of Honor, for his heroic actions at the Battle of Fair Oaks.

He was married to a Bucks County woman, Sara Sigafoos, in 1865. The couple had four children together. At some point, Pursell settled in southern Luzerne County, in the Borough of White Haven, and worked on the Lehigh Valley Railroad as a supervisor on a maintenance crew. He served his adopted community on the school board and the borough council. He died on May 13, 1918, and was interred in the Laurel Cemetery. His grave is located near a marker erected in the 1880s by local veterans of the Civil War.

Gone But Not Forgotten | *Civil War Veterans of Northeastern Pennsylvania*

Color Sergeant Hiram Pursell, Co. G, 104th Pennsylvania Volunteer Infantry, Laurel Cemetery, White Haven
Credit: Kristen Lindbuchler Photo

Isaac E. Severn
1835 – June 21, 1868

Schuylkill County Pennsylvania provided many men to serve the Union cause. Many were employed by the mighty coal industry, the main industry throughout central and northeastern Pennsylvania. One such man was Isaac Severn. He was born in Schuylkill County and made a living as an administrator of a local coal company. In 1859 Severn had a promising career and married a Pottsville, Pennsylvania woman by the name of Matilda. All was going well with the young couple until war erupted in the spring of 1861.

Many men, especially mine laborers, saw an opportunity to leave the backbreaking, dangerous work of coal mining in favor of soldiering. Many regiments were recruited within the county, especially from the city of Pottsville. One such regiment was the 96th Pennsylvania Volunteer Infantry. Severn left his young wife behind and enlisted in Company C on September 2, 1861. Because of his status as a leader within the coal industry, he was immediately given the rank of first lieutenant. Military records indicate that he brought with him a servant to wash clothes, cook, sew, or perform any other chores, which Severn might ask of the man.

The regiment trained on Lawton's Hill overlooking the city of Pottsville for a period of two months, then was sent southward to Washington, issued Harper's Ferry muskets and completed training over the winter of 1861-62. The 96th was attached to the VI Corps in May of 1862 and took part in the various battles of the Peninsula Campaign, including Malvern Hill and Gaines' Mill, taking minor losses. The men of Company C performed admirably under Lieutenant Severn's watchful eye. The regiment next met the enemy in September of 1862 at the Battle of South Mountain, losing a substantial number of men for the first time. It was held in reserve at the Battle of Antietam and lost virtually no men there.

On November 1, 1862, Lieutenant Severn was promoted to the rank of captain and took official command of the company. He retained this command (with only a few interruptions) for the remainder of the regiment's term of service. The regiment next met the enemy at Fredericksburg in December and took part in skirmishing, taking minor losses once more. During the Chancellorsville campaign on May 3, the VI Corps, including the 96th regiment, took possession of Marye's Heights in Fredericksburg and pushed forward to Chancellorsville, losing about eighty men in the operation. Severn led his men with precision, but was in poor health due to a bad case of diarrhea. Because of the poor food quality, poor sanitation, and hard physical exertion, most men suffered this malady, some worse than others. Severn returned home for ten

days leave in March of 1863 in hopes of recovering, but his sickness would not subside.

When the Battle of Gettysburg began on July 1, 1863, the 96th regiment was a full one and one-half days' march from the town and began a grueling march at a fast pace. The men covered a distance of more than thirty miles in practically one day. This quick march nearly killed Severn as he became weak and exhausted from the severe diarrhea, but he made it to the field with his men. The regiment was posted near Little Round Top, taking light casualties. It took part in the pursuit of Lee's army and lost a few men in a skirmish near Hagerstown, Maryland on July 10. Before going into winter camp, the regiment took part in the battles of Bristoe Station and Mine Run.

During the winter of 1863-64, Severn caught a severe cold, which seemed to remain with him, to some extent for the rest of his life. In later pension reports, doctors diagnosed Severn with lung disease and tuberculosis, attributing its origin to Severn's service in the army. In pension records, Severn mentions the persistent cough that had remained with him since he was afflicted with the severe cold.

In May of 1864, the Army of the Potomac, under newly-appointed General Ulysses S. Grant, began the task of destroying Lee's army and capturing Richmond. This task began with the Battle of the Wilderness. The 96th took part in the confused skirmishing and lost its Corps commander, Major General John Sedgwick, who was killed by a Confederate sharpshooter. On May 10, 1864, the regiment assaulted a strong Confederate position at Spotsylvania Court House, losing 178 men out of 350 engaged. Again, Severn led his men in these bloody battles, coming out of both unscathed.

In June, the regiment assaulted the Confederate fortifications at Cold Harbor, Virginia, again suffering heavy losses among the men that remained. It was next assigned the task of building fortifications in front of the Confederate-held city of Petersburg, and then was sent to the Shenandoah Valley to stop a Confederate force under General Jubal Early from invading Washington. On September 22, the term of service for the regiment expired, and it was sent northward to Baltimore, Harrisburg, and then Pottsville, where it was welcomed back with great enthusiasm. Most men were paid and mustered out in West Philadelphia on October 21, 1864. Others, who had enlisted after 1861, were reassigned to the 95th Pennsylvania Volunteer Infantry and remained with the army.

Severn returned home to Pottsville a frail and weak man. The years of campaigning had taken their toll on Severn, and he looked to be much older than he was. After attempting a short recovery, he began his duties as the paymaster of the Suffolk Coal Company and moved to Mahanoy City, Pennsylvania in 1865. The couple began a family when Matilda gave birth to a daughter, Minnie, in February of 1866. Still bothered by a persistent cough and diarrhea, Severn's health steadily worsened. On June 21, 1868, three months after the birth of his second child, Katie, Severn died at his home in Mahanoy City. The family physician attributed the death to bleeding of the lungs, from excessive coughing and dehydration from the effects of severe diarrhea.

Sadly, in April of the following year, the couple's first daughter Minnie died of unknown causes. Her sister, Katie, died in 1884, again due to unknown causes. Mrs. Matilda Severn was left alone, dying in Mahanoy City in 1914 of disease. Modern medicine, which we perhaps take for granted, would most likely have saved the lives of this family. The final resting place of the entire family can be found at the Presbyterian Cemetery in Pottsville.

Captain Isaac Severn and family, Co. C, 96th Pennsylvania Volunteer Infantry
Credit: U.S. Army Military History Institute Collection

ANDREW LAPE
February 5, 1837 – April 16, 1862

Mr. and Mrs. Adam Lape had seven children through the course of their marriage. The family owned a farm near the town of Nanticoke, Pennsylvania, and lived an average middle-class life. The third child, Andrew Lape, was born at the family homestead on a cold February day in 1837. Lape, as described by his mother, Elizabeth, was a shy, pensive boy who was very attached to his mother. This was in sharp contrast to his two other brothers, Franklin and William, who were free spirited boys who loved to get into mischief.

Lape led a normal childhood until the death of his father in 1847. The family got by under the tight purse strings of Elizabeth and the children got a decent education at the common schools of Nanticoke. When Civil War broke out in 1861, Lape, perhaps tired of the life of a farmer, decided to join the army. He and his brother William traveled to Wilkes-Barre in September of 1861 and enlisted in the 9th Pennsylvania Volunteer Cavalry, or the "Lochiel Cavalry." They joined Company D of the regiment and were soon sent southward to the state capital at Harrisburg where the regiment took up residence at Camp Cameron. It was here that Lape wrote home to his mother describing how well the regiment was supplied with provisions:

> We have plenty to eat and drink. We live on bread, crackers, smoked shoulder, fresh beef, beans, rice, potatoes, sugar, coffee. We have candles, soap, vinegar, salt and pepper…..

In the letter, he went on to tell his mother that he would be sending home his pay in order to support his family, and mentioned that his brother William was doing fine.

The regiment was drilled at Camp Cameron and then sent by rail to Pittsburgh, then by boat to Louisville, Kentucky. It was sent to Jefferson, Indiana to be placed under the command of General Don Carlos Buell. During the late months of 1861 the regiment was outfitted with horses and commenced mounted drill. Having grown up on a farm with horses made it easy for Lape to master these skills. In January of 1862, the regiment had acquired the necessary skills and was transferred to the front at Kentucky. The regiment was split into three battalions (groups of companies), with Lape's battalion being sent to Grayson Springs to protect the citizens from Confederate troops under Confederate General Albert Sidney Johnston.

On March 5, his battalion was ordered to Springfield, Tennessee. While there, Lape fell ill with a fever. During the Civil War, many more men died from illness than from battle wounds. This was because there were no vaccinations against diseases such as measles, chicken pox, etc. Urban recruits, who had had more exposure to such diseases, enjoyed greater immunity than rural recruits, such as Lape. Since there was essentially no effective treatment, many died from common everyday diseases that modern medicine has eliminated.

Lape was diagnosed with typhoid fever and died at the hospital in Springfield on April 16, 1862. His mother received the sad news from her other son William who had served alongside Lape during his brief military career. William continued to serve with the regiment and survived many battles, such as Murfreesboro, Perryville and Chickamauga, attaining the rank of sergeant. Elizabeth received a pension of $8 per month from the government for the loss of her son and continued to collect until her death. Lape's other brother Franklin served as a substitute in Company D of the 61st Pennsylvania Volunteer Infantry from October, 1864, to June, 1865.

William was another Lape that became a victim of disease, dying in December of 1876 from tuberculosis. Andrew and William Lape are buried at the Hanover Green Cemetery where one may visit their graves today. Franklin's final resting place is a mystery.

JAMES J. MAYCOCK
May 22, 1826 – December 9, 1884

James Maycock was born in Great Britain. He came to the United States with a new bride, Sarah, before the Civil War broke out. The couple was married on March 28, 1857, and Sarah eventually bore her husband five children. When war broke out in 1861, James was employed as a bricklayer in Scranton and lived on Wyoming Avenue. A year went by and Maycock perhaps felt a patriotic duty to his adopted country and decided to enlist in the Army in August, 1862.

The Governor of Pennsylvania, Andrew Curtin, had recently called for the raising of several nine-month regiments to serve the Union cause. Maycock enlisted in Scranton on August 9, at the age of thirty-six. On the muster rolls he is listed as being 5'5", having brown hair, blue eyes, and a dark complexion. He enlisted in Company I of the 132nd Pennsylvania Volunteer Infantry Regiment. Company I was known as the "Railroad Guards" and its men were predominantly from the city of Scranton, within Luzerne County. At that time, modern-day Lackawanna County did not exist, and it was a part of Luzerne County.

Leaving his young wife behind, Maycock was transported with the regiment to Fort Corcoran, near Washington, D.C., in order to be trained as a soldier. In September, the regiment was attached to the third division of the II Corps, Army of the Potomac. It joined the corps just in time to take part in some of the hardest fighting of the war. The regiment reached the field of battle at South Mountain on September 13 after marching thirty-three miles. It was only lightly engaged, but would meet the enemy again on September 17 at Antietam Creek, Maryland.

The regiment was ordered to the portion of the field known as the "sunken road." This road was so well used by the local population that it was sunken into the earth and was a natural fortification for defending troops. Confederate forces occupied the road and waited for the Union troops to assault. As the II Corps, including the 132nd, was ordered toward the road, several beehives were upset. Angry bees soon attacked the green recruits of the 132nd. This caused some confusion, but it was quickly resolved. The regiment was ordered to attack the well-fortified Confederate position in the sunken road. The fighting was furious as the Union troops attempted to capture the road. The men were eventually able to capture the position, but at a frightful cost to both sides. The Confederates defending the road were driven off, leaving the road full of dead and dying. The field in front of the road, where the Union troops assaulted was also filled with the dead and wounded. The 132nd Pennsylvania Infantry lost 148 men, including its beloved Colonel, Richard Oakford, whose remains lie in the Hollenback Cemetery in Wilkes-Barre.

Private James Maycock was also among the wounded on that terrible day. During the assault on the position, a Confederate musket ball had struck Maycock in the left side of his lower jaw. The bullet entered the jawbone, destroying molars, and passed through his mouth under the tongue, resting in the right side of his jawbone, destroying the molars there as well. Maycock was removed from the field and a large portion of his lower jawbone was removed, resulting in a great deformity. He was transported to a hospital in Reading, Pennsylvania, to rest and recuperate. He remained in this hospital until his discharge from the Army on May 24, 1863.

Upon his return to Scranton, Maycock resumed his trade as a bricklayer and the couple had five children in the years that followed (Bertha – 1872, James – 1874, Walter – 1877, Edward – 1880, and Grace – 1883). Those years were painful ones for Maycock. According to pension records, his wound never really healed correctly, causing much pain and a serious deformity. He also complained that he could not masticate, or chew, food effectively, resulting in frequent indigestion. In 1866, he was awarded a $6 per month pension for his disability.

On December 9, 1884, Maycock died from an infection caused by his wound. The examining physician called it "a disease of the brain caused by the wound." Even though he lived twenty-two years after he was wounded, one can consider him mortally wounded at the battle of Antietam. His remains lie in the Forrest Hill Cemetery in Scranton. Sarah Maycock joined her husband in eternal rest in 1921.

Gone But Not Forgotten | *Civil War Veterans of Northeastern Pennsylvania*

Private James J. Maycock, Co. I, 132ND Pennsylvania Volunteer Infantry
Credit: G.A.R. Post 139 Collection

John S. Short
April 10, 1841 – November 15, 1899

In August, 1862, the Civil War had been going on for more than a year. The Union cause was no closer to victory in the east than it was in April, 1861. Pennsylvania had already sent over one hundred regiments to serve the cause, but more regiments were needed to defeat the enemy. Governor Andrew Curtin called for several nine-month regiments to be recruited for service. The 132nd Pennsylvania Volunteer Infantry Regiment was to be made up of men from several counties of northeastern Pennsylvania. Companies I and K would come from Luzerne County, which at that time included the area of modern-day Lackawanna County. Recruiting commenced in Scranton and the ranks filled quickly.

One of those recruits, John S. Short, was a twenty year-old clerk who was born in Ashley, Pennsylvania, but now lived in Scranton. He enlisted in Company K (the "Scranton Guards") on August 9, and received a $25 bounty. The regiment was sent south to Washington, D.C., to be instructed in the art of war. In early September, the regiment took the field with the third division of the II Corps, Army of the Potomac. The regiment came under fire for the first time on September 13, at the Battle of South Mountain, but the fighting was light by the time the 132nd got there. Four days later the regiment would meet the enemy again, this time on the bloodiest day in American history, at Antietam, Maryland.

The regiment fought bravely at Antietam, taking part in the assault on the "sunken road." The regiment took heavy casualties and performed like veterans instead of green recruits. Short survived unhurt but observed many of his friends go down wounded or dead. Perhaps Short wondered what his fate would be in the next eight months. He was promoted to the rank of corporal on September 24. (The following December, the Army was placed under the command of Major General Ambrose Burnside, who was itching to punish the Confederate Army.)

On December 13, the Confederate Army had positioned itself behind a stone wall at the foot of a large hill by the name of "Marye's Heights," in the town of Fredericksburg, Virginia. Atop the hill were positioned several batteries which laid a devastating fire upon the attacking Federal troops. The regiment took part in the suicidal frontal assaults ordered by the commanding generals, and performed bravely, losing 150 out of 340 men. Among those wounded was Private John Short. During one of the assaults, an enemy musket ball struck him in the right thigh where the leg meets the hip. The bullet went through the bone, shattering it, causing a frightful exit wound from which particles of bone were protruding. John was taken to a field hospital and then

sent to Washington to Mount Pleasant Hospital in order to recover.

Short spent the next six months in the hospital and was discharged from the Army on May 24, 1863, as the survivors of his original company were being mustered out of the service. His right leg was now four inches shorter than the left, and he could not walk without a crutch. It is unusual that the leg was not amputated, as was common practice by Civil War era surgeons. Medicine of the period was not nearly advanced as it is today. Little was known about preventing infection and treating many types of injuries.

Short returned to Scranton with an Army pension of $8 per month, and attempted to begin a new life as an invalid. His wound caused much pain and forced him to remain bedridden most of the time. He was able to meet and marry a local woman, Lucinda Lotzinger. The two were married in Wilkes-Barre on New Year's Eve, 1864. The couple had three children (Ezra, Nettie, and John) and led a happy life together. Short was able to find a job as a clerk in the tobacco industry, but was severely limited in his activities due to his injury.

By 1890, his pension was increased to $12 per month, but the pain of his wound was relentless. In a letter written to the pension office, Short's doctor stated that he was unable to work much of the time due to the pain, and was forced to remain in bed. The doctor also stated that the wound had opened up several times, causing severe pain and a discharge. Short was released from his pain in 1899, when he died at the family home on Franklin Avenue in Scranton. He was fifty-eight years of age. His remains were laid to rest at the Forrest Hill Cemetery in Scranton.

Ryan Lindbuchler

Corporal John S. Short, Co. K, 132nd Pennsylvania Volunteer Infantry
Credit: G.A.R. Post 139 Collection

MOSES MORRIS
1838-August 17, 1872

For the first two years of the American Civil War, most Northern generals and politicians avoided the use of blacks as soldiers. They felt that blacks were not intelligent or brave enough to fight the enemy in an organized manner. Conversely, most free blacks felt that they should have a right to be a part of the war that would free all their people from the bonds of slavery. They reasoned that if they earned the right of citizenship by fighting and dying for the Union cause, no person could tell them that they were not entitled to all the rights and privileges that white Americans held under the Constitution.

Even with white resistance, the enlistment of blacks into the army was becoming a reality by 1863. The State of Massachusetts, supported by its governor, John Andrew, and a famous black abolitionist and ex-slave, Frederick Douglass, secured permission to raise a colored regiment. Robert Gould Shaw, a veteran officer of the 2nd Massachusetts Volunteer Infantry (a white regiment), and a member of a prominent abolitionist family from Boston, led the 54th Massachusetts as its colonel.

The 54th was one of the first black regiments to be formed in the North and was looked upon with great curiosity by most Northerners. Upon hearing about the formation of the regiment, many free blacks and escaped slaves flocked to Camp Meigs in Readville, Massachusetts, to enlist in the regiment. A free black named Moses Morris, of Lawrence, Pennsylvania, (Clearfield County) heard about the regiment and immediately left his job as a railway porter to make his way north to enlist. He reached Readville by April, 1863, and was mustered in on May 13 as a private in Company D. Company records indicate that he was twenty-seven years of age, 5'8" tall, with a dark complexion, brown eyes, and black hair. He was born in Lancaster, Pennsylvania, and was single when he enlisted.

The regiment trained in camp until the end of the month, then was transferred south for action on the front lines. It arrived at Hilton Head, South Carolina, on June 3 and was engaged with the enemy for the first time on July 16 at James Island in a diversionary attack. The regiment performed beautifully and repulsed a Confederate attack, losing forty-six men. Two weeks earlier, the Union Army of the Potomac had won the battle of Gettysburg in Pennsylvania and turned the war on a course that was in favor of the North. However, there was much interest in the success of the 54th because they were the so-called "litmus test" to learn how blacks would behave in battle. At James Island they proved that they could fight as well as whites, but Colonel

Shaw wanted to prove it in a larger battle with more significant effects.

His chance came two days later when his brigade commander, George C. Strong, offered Shaw the chance to lead an attack on a fort (Battery Wagner) that was guarding the major seaport of Charleston, South Carolina. An assault had been made earlier and met with disaster, but this time Strong felt that the fort had been shelled sufficiently by the U.S. Navy and Army siege guns, and was greatly weakened. About 8 p.m. the 54th attacked the fort with its young colonel leading the charge across the beach and up the parapets of the fort. He was shot down and killed, but the 54th surged forward, taking tremendous casualties and breaching the walls of the fortress. In this attack Private Morris was hit in the left hand by an enemy minié ball. The ball lodged in the palm of his hand, making it useless and causing great pain. He was also struck in the right side by a piece of shrapnel, but was able to escape through the carnage in front of the fort back to the Federal position, and watched as the men of his regiment melted away in the parapets of Battery Wagner.

Even though the men reached the inside of the fort, the garrison was too strong and the 54th was driven out, losing 250 men that night. The fort was never taken, and Colonel Shaw lay dead on the beach and General Strong mortally wounded, along with hundreds of other fallen heroes. The ball was removed from Morris' hand, and he was sent to the army hospital at Beaufort, South Carolina, until November, then sent to David's Island, New York, finally ending up at New Haven, Connecticut. He was sent back to his regiment in May, 1864 with very limited movement in the fingers of his left hand and a peculiar cough that had materialized during his hospital confinement.

The attack on the fort, along with the heroic death of Colonel Shaw, had made the 54th a famous regiment and gave it a reputation as the best colored regiment serving with the army. As a result, many other colored regiments began to be recruited throughout the North. Eventually, over 100,000 blacks would enlist in the U.S. Army. When Morris reached his regiment, it was stationed in Florida and took part in the Battle of Olustee. The 54th, along with another colored regiment, the 35th U.S., was responsible for saving the Union force by serving as a rearguard. It lost eighty-six men in the battle, and this time Morris was not among the wounded.

The regiment returned to Morris Island (near Charleston) where it remained until November, 1864. It was engaged at the Battle of Honey Hill where it lost forty-two men. It was sent to Pocotaligo, South Carolina, to act as guards for Major General William T. Sherman's base of supplies in February, 1865, and finally entered the city of Charleston on November 27. On March 27 it was engaged with the enemy at Boydkin's Mill on a raid into the interior of the state of South Carolina, taking light casualties. Morris took part in all this activity and remained uninjured. The regiment was mustered out of service at Mount Pleasant, South Carolina, on August 20, 1865, and was transported north to Boston, reviewed by Governor Andrew, and disbanded on August 28.

Morris returned to Pennsylvania, this time to his hometown of Lancaster. He took a job as a laborer, but it was difficult work because his hand had very limited movement and caused him much pain at times. His income was supplemented with a government pension of $5 per month for the wound.

While he was living in Lancaster, he met Sara J. Brown, who was visiting from Wilkes-Barre, Pennsylvania. A courtship began and the two were married on December 1, 1869. The couple moved to Hudson Street in Wilkes-Barre in 1870, where Morris again resumed work as a laborer. The peculiar cough that Morris had contracted while in the hospitals after his wounding, began to

worsen and the couple feared that Morris might have tuberculosis. This disease had no treatment in this period and was basically a death sentence for any person who was stricken. It was simply a matter of time before breathing became impossible because the victims' lungs slowly filled with fluids, suffocating them from within.

Morris lasted two years and passed away on August 17, 1872, almost seven years to the day of his discharge from the army. Morris was buried in the Wilkes-Barre City Cemetery, close to many other black men who had served the Union and earned the right of citizenship through blood and fire. Sara moved to New York City by 1878 and was granted a widow's pension of $8 per month in 1891 and $30 per month in 1924. She died in Wilkes-Barre on August 6, 1924.

CORPORAL MOSES MORRIS, CO. D, 54TH MASSACHUSETTS VOLUNTEER INFANTRY, WILKES-BARRE CITY CEMETERY
CREDIT: KRISTEN LINDBUCHLER PHOTO

ROBERT BRUCE RICKETTS
April 29, 1839 – November 13, 1918

Robert Bruce Ricketts was born the fifth son of Elijah and Margaret Ricketts in the small Columbia County town of Orangeville. The Ricketts were of Scottish descent, and Robert was the grandson of a Revolutionary War officer who served under Colonel Davidson in the Pennsylvania Militia. Robert led an average middle class life and was studying to become a lawyer in 1861 at the age of twenty-two.

Perhaps adventure called to Ricketts when he enlisted on July 8 as a private in Captain Matthews' Battery F of the 1st Pennsylvania Light Artillery. His leadership skills were quickly observed, and Ricketts was commissioned a lieutenant of Battery F only one month after enlisting. By the fall of 1861, the regiment had received its training and the batteries were scattered throughout the various divisions of the Union Army, as was common practice during the period. Battery F was attached to the V Corps in September, 1861, under the command of Nathaniel P. Banks.

Lieutenant Ricketts was in command of his section of the battery when it first came under fire at a skirmish in December and performed perfectly. The battery was transferred to the I Corps and served at the battles of Dranesville, Bunker Hill, Newtown, Cedar Mountain, Second Bull Run, Antietam, and Fredericksburg. The regiment served valiantly, losing many men along the way. On March 14, 1863, as the Corps was preparing to begin the spring campaign, Captain Matthews was promoted to major and Lieutenant Ricketts took command of the Battery.

The newly named "Ricketts' Battery" performed well at the Battle of Chancellorsville in early May, 1863 and Lieutenant Ricketts was promoted to captain on May 8. The greatest test for the Battery and Captain Ricketts occurred at the Battle of Gettysburg on the evening of July 2, 1863. Captain Ricketts' command, including Battery G of the same regiment, was posted in an exposed position on East Cemetery Hill. He had orders to hold his position at all costs. This was because his command was posted at the Union center and a Confederate breakthrough could result in disaster for the Union army.

In late afternoon, Ricketts observed a large Confederate force made up of 1,700 men of five Louisiana "Tiger" Zouave regiments massing for an attack in his front. With the famous "rebel yell," the Tigers began to charge the position. The Union Infantry of the XI Corps that was detailed to support the battery fled in dismay, leaving Ricketts' Battery alone to face the fury of the attackers. Immediately, Ricketts ordered his men to fire grapeshot, or canister, at the attacking troops. Canister ammunition, when fired, can be considered shotgun-like because it is

essentially a can containing large iron balls that spread over a large area, causing massive damage to whatever is hit. It is effective to only about 300 or 400 yards but was the ammunition of choice for gunners who were attempting to repulse an infantry or cavalry attack. According to Bates' *History of Pennsylvania Volunteers*, when Captain Ricketts saw fear in a few of his men's faces, he responded with determination. Bates wrote, "With an iron hand Ricketts kept every man to his post and every gun in full play." (Volume II, 963)

The Tigers were massacred in front of Ricketts' guns, but a substantial number managed to overrun the battery in an attempt to spike Ricketts' guns. His men replied with a furious counterattack, using handspikes, gun-swabs, stones, and fists. One unfortunate Confederate tried to capture the guidon (small silk triangular flag) of the battery and was beaten to death by one of Ricketts' men. Currently, the Luzerne County Historical Society possesses this guidon in their collection and displays it on occasion. Just in the nick of time, infantrymen were rushed up to support the battery and the survivors of Hays' Louisiana Tigers were driven from the field. The beaten force originally left Confederate lines with 1,700 men and returned with barely 600.

Following Gettysburg, the battery served heroically in many of the bloodiest battles of the spring campaign of 1864. It was engaged at Bristoe Station, Wilderness, Cold Harbor, and Petersburg. On December 1, 1864, Ricketts was promoted to the rank of major and given entire command of the artillery of the IX Corps, Army of the Potomac. In March, 1865, he was promoted again, this time to the rank of colonel of the 1st Pennsylvania Light Artillery. He served in this capacity until the cessation of hostilities and was honorably discharged on June 3, 1865.

Ricketts returned to northeastern Pennsylvania and settled in Wilkes-Barre. He decided not to resume his law studies and was able to invest in large tracts of heavily wooded land on the North Mountain, in the counties of Sullivan, Wyoming, and Luzerne. He, along with other investors, began a lucrative lumber business. At the age of 28, Ricketts was married in Wilkes-Barre on October 1, 1868, to Elizabeth Reynolds of Kingston, Pennsylvania. The couple had two daughters and one son. They made their residence at 80-84 S. River St. in Wilkes-Barre, a mansion which still stands today.

In 1886, Ricketts was persuaded to run for lieutenant governor, but was unsuccessful. In 1898, he was appointed Receiver of Taxes for the city of Wilkes-Barre and served in this capacity with great accomplishment until 1902. In his post-war years he was very active in various social organizations and was somewhat of a local personality in northeastern Pennsylvania. He was a member of the Wyoming Historical and Geological Society, the Grand Army of the Republic Post 97, Military Order of the Loyal Legion, Pennsylvania Gettysburg Monument Commission, Westmoreland Club, Fraternity of Free and Accepted Masons and the Knights Templar of Wilkes-Barre.

In addition to the family home in Wilkes-Barre, the Ricketts' built a home at Lake Ganoga on North Mountain. It was used frequently by the family as a secondary home, and the couple preferred to stay at this location more and more frequently as they grew old together. On November 13, 1918, two days after the United States had defeated the Central Powers of World War I, Colonel Robert Bruce Ricketts died at the family home at Lake Ganoga. Suffering from a long illness and perhaps heartbroken because of the loss of her husband, Elizabeth Ricketts died at the family home in Wilkes-Barre six days later. The couple was buried near Lake Ganoga on the North Mountain at a private family plot where their remains lie today. Much of the land once owned by Ricketts was donated to the state for the purpose of creating a public park. That park bears its benefactor's name, Ricketts' Glen State Park.

Gone But Not Forgotten | *Civil War Veterans of Northeastern Pennsylvania*

CAPTAIN ROBERT B. RICKETTS, BATTERY F, 1ST PENNSYLVANIA VOLUNTEER LIGHT ARTILLERY
CREDIT: U.S. ARMY MILITARY HISTORY INSTITUTE COLLECTION

SYLVESTER DANA RHODES
December 6, 1842 – August 29, 1904

Sylvester D. Rhodes was born to a middle-class family in the Borough of Parsons (then Plains Township) near Wilkes-Barre. Rhodes attended the common schools of Plains and anticipated an average life in the Wyoming Valley. In 1861 the Civil War would change those expectations. Like many of his friends, Rhodes saw his chance to serve the Union and enlisted at the age of nineteen. He joined the 8th Pennsylvania Volunteer Infantry Regiment, a ninety-day regiment called up by Governor Curtin to serve the Commonwealth. He served as a private in Company F, which had been a militia company before the war. They were known as the "Wyoming Artillerists," and were originally located at Wyoming, Pennsylvania.

The regiment had a rather uneventful term of service under the command of General William Patterson, and was mustered out on July 29, 1861. Rhodes almost immediately joined another regiment, the 23rd Pennsylvania Volunteer Infantry Regiment, also known as Birney's Zouaves. Zouaves were troops that were outfitted with intricate and fanciful uniforms patterned after French troops who served in Africa in the years before the American Civil War. The training and equipment of these Zouaves were essentially the same as other Federal regiments and many, like the 23rd, were issued standard army pattern uniforms when the Zouave uniforms were worn out. Rhodes served in Company L, made up of Luzerne County men, from September 1861, until March 1862, when he was transferred to the 61st Pennsylvania Volunteer Infantry Regiment. By July of that year, he was promoted to the rank of sergeant in Company D.

With the rest of the regiment, Rhodes served with the IV, then the VI Corps in the Army of the Potomac. The regiment saw action in all the major engagements of that army. The regiment was engaged at Falling Waters, Yorktown, Fair Oaks, Malvern Hill, Antietam, Salem Heights, Williamsport, Fredericksburg, Gettysburg, Marye's Heights (1863), Rappahannock Station, and the Wilderness. On May 11, 1864 at the Battle of Yellow Tavern, Rhodes was wounded near the base of the spine and was taken to City Point hospital where he was to recover. He rejoined his regiment on September 15 and led the company at the battles of Winchester, Fisher's Hill, and Cedar Creek.

At the Battle of Fisher's Hill on September 22, 1864, Rhodes served as captain and lead the company in that engagement. It was here that he would distinguish himself as a courageous and daring leader. According to the book, <u>Deeds of Valor</u>, Company D engaged the enemy, sheltered behind breastworks. The Confederates behind the breastworks directed Confederate artillery fire on advancing columns of Federal troops. Stepping in front of his company, Sergeant Rhodes pointed beyond the breastworks at the artillery and exclaimed, "Now boys, let's go for those guns!" (422) The Company surged forward into enemy fire, inspiring the Color Company of the regiment (Company F) to follow. The rest of the regiment followed, and the result was absolute victory. Company D was the first to overrun the breastworks and take the guns. Sergeant Rhodes and his men immediately loaded a piece and fired into the backs of the fleeing enemy. The company captured seventeen guns and drove the enemy from its formidable position under the inspiring leadership of Sylvester Rhodes. In 1897, Rhodes received the highest honor that can be bestowed upon an American soldier, the Medal of Honor.

After Fisher's Hill, Rhodes took part in the siege and capture of Petersburg, and the battles of Farmville and Appomattox, eventually attaining the rank of captain of Company D in April of 1865. He returned home briefly in order to marry Susan Huffman of Plains on May 12, 1865. He was mustered out on June 28, 1865 with the rest of the 61st Infantry.

Rhodes returned home to start a family and begin a career in engineering. Together the couple had six children: John S. (1867); Fred C. (1868); Charles S. (1871); Allan O. (1873); Daisy B. (1875); and Paul B. (1878). Along with his career in stationary engineering and as an inspector with the Wilkes-Barre Water Works, Rhodes served with the Coal and Iron Police during the riots of 1869-70. He served as a lieutenant in Company E, 9th Regiment, Pennsylvania National Guard between 1883 and 1885 and also remained active in the local post of the Grand Army of the Republic in Wilkes-Barre.

Sylvester D. Rhodes personified the word "courage" by his actions in the greatest battles of the Civil War. After suffering for many years from "muscular atrophy" as a result of the spinal wound he sustained at the Battle of Yellow Tavern, he died at the family home in Parsons forty years after the battle. He is laid to rest at the Hollenback Cemetery in Wilkes-Barre, with a simple government stone to serve as his memorial.

Captain Sylvester D. Rhodes, Co. D, 61st Pennsylvania Volunteer Infantry
Credit: Ryan Lindbuchler Photo

WELLINGTON H. ENT
August 18, 1834 – November 5, 1871

Wellington Ent was born the son of Peter Ent in Lightstreet, Pennsylvania. Wellington was one of four sons and planned to follow in his father's footsteps as a lawyer. As a youngster, Ent attended common schools at Williamsport, Pennsylvania, and graduated from Dickinson Seminary in 1858. He then studied law at Bloomsburg and later the University at Albany, New York. He was admitted to the bar in September of 1860, at the age of twenty-six. He served as a Notary Public in Bloomsburg until his country called him to do his duty in 1861.

With the call for volunteers being issued by President Lincoln, and Confederate forces capturing Fort Sumter in Charleston, South Carolina, ten days earlier, a recruiting frenzy occurred in the Town of Bloomsburg. Because of his reputation as an outstanding citizen, Ent was commissioned first lieutenant of Company A of the 35th Pennsylvania Volunteer Infantry. The 35th would quickly be designated the 6th Pennsylvania Reserves, in accordance with Governor Andrew Curtin's call for a reserve corps made up of Pennsylvania men. Company A was made up of men from Bloomsburg and called itself the "Iron Guard." It was led by Captain William Ricketts, who would be commissioned colonel of the regiment by July of 1861.

The Regiment was mustered into service at Harrisburg in May, 1861. Promotions were given the following month, and Lieutenant Ent was promoted to captain of Company A. Before leaving Harrisburg the regiment was trained in the manual of arms and Company A was issued the new Springfield rifles (model 1861). The regiment was next transported to Washington, where it was attached to the third brigade of General McCall's Division.

In August of that year Captain Ent was temporarily attached to the U.S. Signal Corps for limited duty, and returned to his men by the following September. The regiment received its baptism by fire at the Battle of Dranesville in December of 1861, where it was detailed to perform reconnaissance. It was during this battle that Captain Ent was struck in the heel by an enemy bullet. Luckily, it only carried away part of his boot, and not his foot. The regiment remained in winter camp for the next three months and Captain Ent was able to train his company to ready them for the coming campaign.

In June, the regiment was transferred to the V Corps where it would remain for the remainder of its service. During much of General McClellan's Peninsula Campaign, the 6th was ordered to remain behind the lines to guard supplies. But the following August it was engaged at the Battle of Second Bull Run where it lost forty-four men. Only a few weeks later, Captain Ent

would again lead his men into battle at South Mountain where Companies A and B were able to dislodge the well-fortified enemy and drive them from the mountainside. Only three days later, the regiment would find itself again on the field of battle, this time at Antietam Creek on September 17, 1862. The regiment took part in the repulse of Confederate troops advancing through the now famous Miller Cornfield and sustained considerable loss in the action, losing 132 men. Because of the high turnover rate of regimental command and his courageous leadership, Captain Ent was promoted to major on September 21, but had been acting in that capacity since shortly before the Battle of Antietam.

In November, the resignation of Lieutenant Colonel McKean meant that Major Ent was to command the entire regiment. He commanded the regiment through the blood and carnage of the Battle of Fredericksburg, where the regiment again lost heavily. It was detached to perform guard duty with the XXII Corps from February until June of 1863 and missed the Battle of Chancellorsville. Major Ent was promoted to lieutenant colonel on May 1 and retained command of the regiment. The 6th was again attached to the V Corps and took part in the Battle of Gettysburg at the Little Round Top portion of the field on July 2, 1863, where it took minimal losses. Lieutenant Colonel Ent was again promoted, this time to colonel, on July 1, 1863. He led the regiment through several more engagements in the fall and winter of 1863 including Bristoe Station, New Hope Church, and Mine Run. Each time the regiment performed very well and was known for its proficiency in drill under Ent's command, who escaped unhurt each time.

Winter quarters were spent near Kettle-Run, and the regiment was able to rest and recuperate from a year of hard-fought battles. It served valiantly at the Battle of the Wilderness in May of 1864 and Colonel Ent was assigned command of the third brigade of the division. Under his command, the brigade (composed of three to five regiments) performed courageously and sustained substantial losses during assaults on Confederate fortifications at Spotsylvania Court House. Colonel Ent led his men in battle at Bethesda Church on May 30 and was wounded in the action. He received a wound to the hand and was carried from the field by ambulance to a nearby field hospital.

Upon his recovery, he was assigned to various duties with the Army of the Potomac, serving as a paymaster at one point. He was mustered out with the regiment on June 11, 1864. He returned to Bloomsburg and resumed his law practice, awaiting the return of two of his brothers who had volunteered for service. His brother Robert served as a lieutenant in the 178th Pennsylvania Infantry, and Usal had served as a lieutenant in the 84th Pennsylvania Infantry. The following March, Ent learned that he had been promoted to brigadier general in recognition of "valiant conduct at the Battle of the Wilderness" in 1864.

Ent served as an attorney in Bloomsburg and was elected Prothonotary and clerk of Columbia County Court in 1869. He was also married that same year to Mary E. Petrikin and had one daughter, Anna, who was born on May 14, 1870. Anna would marry in her mid twenties and die at the age of twenty-six due to complications during the birth of her first child, who would die as well. Ent would have a similar fate and die in 1871 of unknown causes at the early age of thirty-seven. The general, who had two horses shot out from under him during the war, was laid to rest at the Rosemont Cemetery, where his remains lie today, along with his wife Mary and daughter Anna.

Gone But Not Forgotten | *Civil War Veterans of Northeastern Pennsylvania*

COLONEL WELLINGTON H. ENT, STAFF, 6TH PENNSYLVANIA RESERVES
CREDIT: ROGER D. HUNT COLLECTION

The Tubbs Brothers

Daniel A. Tubbs
1838 - June 19, 1865

Elias Tubbs
1839 – October 28, 1864

Josiah E. Tubbs
1843 - August 21, 1864

Joseph P. Tubbs
1844 – October 30, 1864

Many families were devastated by the loss of loved ones during the Civil War. However, few families suffered as much as the Tubbs family of Fairmount Township in Luzerne County. When Earl and Rebecca sent their four sons off to war, they could never have imagined the outcome that would befall them.

By all indications, the Tubbs family owned a farm in Fairmount Township. All four of the sons of Earl and Rebecca followed in their father's footsteps and became farmers as well. When the Civil War began in 1861, the brothers did not participate in the initial call to arms that took place in the North following President Lincoln's call for state volunteers. Daniel, the oldest of the brothers, was married four years earlier to a local woman named Felicianna Keck in Fairmount Township. By the opening of the war, the couple had two children: William (two years old), and Eveline (one year old).

The second oldest brother, Elias, was married about eighteen months to another local woman, Elizabeth Blain. She had given birth to a daughter, Elizabeth, in November of 1860. The young family owned their own farm near Elias' parents in Fairmount Township. The third brother, Josiah, was married after the beginning of hostilities in August, 1861 to another local woman named Damey (last name unknown). The youngest brother, Joseph, was not married and was living with his parents in 1861.

All four brothers remained civilians through 1861, but this would not be the case in 1862. Joseph, the youngest brother, volunteered for service in March, 1862 in Company K of the 7th Pennsylvania Reserves. Upon his enlistment, the twenty-year-old farmer is listed as having hazel

eyes, dark hair, a light complexion, and standing 5'8" in height. Joseph was sworn into service at Harrisburg in May, 1862 and joined the rest of the regiment just in time to take part in the latest attempt by the Union army to capture the Confederate capital at Richmond, Virginia. The attempt would be called the Peninsula Campaign, and was led by General George B. McClellan. Joseph would receive his baptism by fire at Mechanicsville in June and survived the battle unscathed. He took part in many other battles with the regiment that summer including Gaines' Mill, New Market Crossroads, and Second Bull Run in August.

Back home, Joseph's letters were received by his family and eagerly read by his parents and brothers. Perhaps he sent them the photograph that is included in this book. As Joseph was taking part in the close of the Peninsula Campaign, two of his brothers, Josiah and Elias, joined a local regiment raised by Wilkes-Barre lawyer and Mexican War veteran, Edmund L. Dana. The regiment, the 143rd Pennsylvania Volunteers, trained in the modern-day Borough of Luzerne (at Camp Luzerne). Both brothers left their wives and children and joined Company I of the regiment on September 9, 1862.

On September 14, 1862, Joseph's regiment was engaged in another Battle at South Mountain, Maryland. On the day of the battle, Joseph's company commander reported Joseph missing. He did return in time to take part in the action in the cornfield at Antietam three days later, but was charged with an unauthorized absence and court-martialed on October 1, 1862. He offered no explanation for his absence and plead guilty to one charge, was found guilty, and was fined $10 and returned to duty. It was entirely possible that he had fallen behind on the grueling march that preceded the Battle of South Mountain and had not yet caught up with the regiment when it went into action that day.

Back home, Josiah (about twenty years old) enlisted in the 143rd under the name Earl J. Tubbs, presumably substituting his first name for his middle name. His brother Elias was twenty-three upon his enlistment and stood at 5'8", with a dark complexion, brown eyes, and dark hair. The brothers said goodbye to their families in November and were sent to Harrisburg, then to Washington, to go into winter quarters and train until the opening of the spring campaign in 1863. Perhaps the three brothers met while in winter camp during this time. The 143rd and the 7th served in the I and V Corps respectively, but it would not have been difficult for the brothers to find each other. With only a few exceptions, Civil War armies remained relatively dormant during winter months.

In January, 1863, Joseph was sent on detail to the ambulance train to serve as a driver until March. In April, Josiah was saddened to learn of the death of his five-week-old daughter, Emma, whom he had never seen. The nature of her death is unknown. After the failure of the infamous "mud march" as ordered by General Ambrose Burnside, the Army of the Potomac broke winter camp in the spring and first engaged the enemy at the Battle of Chancellorsville in May. The new commander of the army was Joseph "Fighting Joe" Hooker. The 143rd took part in the action, sustaining considerable loss. Both Josiah and Elias survived with no injury, but the Union army was defeated once again, and morale was very low.

In June, 1863, Confederate forces under Robert E. Lee began the invasion of the North, culminating in the Gettysburg Campaign. Once again, the Army of the Potomac received a new commander, General George G. Meade. Josiah and Elias took part in the action at Gettysburg in July, and miraculously survived without an injury. The 143rd took staggering casualties, including their color-bearer, Benjamin Crippen, and 251 other men, making up over half of the number of men that went into battle. The losses were not in vain however, as the Union cause won a great victory, turning the tide of war in favor of the Union.

Joseph was with his regiment at Alexandria, Virginia, and did not take part in the action at Gettysburg. The 7th Reserves had taken so many casualties during the Peninsula Campaign, the Antietam Campaign, and the Fredericksburg Campaign, that it was sent there to rest and receive recruits for the summer. For the remainder of 1863, both armies avoided battle, attempting to lick their wounds sustained at Gettysburg. During the months of September and October, Joseph was confined to the hospital due to severe diarrhea, but returned to his regiment in decent health by November of 1863.

The winter of 1863-4 would be spent by both regiments in winter encampment once again. In November, Elias was promoted to the rank of corporal. Back at home, the year had been a hard one, as their parents, Earl and Rebecca, and the wives of Josiah and Elias, apprehensively awaited news of the fate of the young men as news of battle after battle reached them. Local newspapers printed long lists of casualties sustained in these battles. Luckily, the names did not appear. As the year 1864 approached, the Tubbs family braced itself for a year of campaigning that would result in the deaths of thousands of young men. Hopefully for them the name "Tubbs" would not be seen.

In March of 1864, Joseph returned home on furlough for thirty days. It would be the last time he was ever seen alive by his family. He returned to his regiment in time to take part in the spring campaign. General Ulysses S. Grant was given command of all Union forces and hoped to defeat Lee's army that summer. The campaign began with the Battle of the Wilderness in May. Both regiments were now part of the same corps and the three brothers fought in the same area during the several days of fighting that ensued. The 7th Reserves was cut off from the rest of the army during the fighting, and most of the regiment was forced to surrender to the enemy. Joseph managed to escape with the remaining survivors, but the regiment was virtually destroyed.

The 143rd lost many men in the fighting as well. As Elias and Josiah fought side-by-side during the battle, both were wounded and became separated. Unable to escape, Josiah fell into the hands of the enemy, and was sent south in the weeks following the battle to the southern prison camp at Andersonville, Georgia. This place was perhaps the most infamous prison of the Civil War, housing thousands of Federal prisoners who suffered under the intense Georgia sun while receiving little or no food rations. Fresh water was scarce and dozens died per day. Josiah, among many of his comrades of the 143rd, survived only about three months. The horrible conditions he was exposed to, along with the effects of his wound, drove him to his death on August 20, 1864. His parents and wife Damey were unaware of his whereabouts since receiving news that he was listed as missing in action by his brother Elias and anxiously awaited news of his fate. For the time being, Elias was safe, as he was sent to City Point, Virginia, to recuperate from his wound.

To make matters worse, Earl and Rebecca learned of the death of their son Joseph in June of 1864. He was killed in action at Bethesda Church on May 30, 1864. The nature of his wound is lost to history, but he was killed instantly while serving with the survivors of the 7th Reserves, only two weeks before he was to be mustered out of service and return home.

While Elias was at City Point recovering, the family gave their last son to the Union cause. Daniel, the oldest of the brothers, had decided to join in the fight. In September of 1864, he left his wife Felicianna and three children (William – six, Eveline – four, and Joseph – one) to join Company D of the 199th Pennsylvania Volunteer Infantry Regiment. His motivations are not known. Perhaps he felt he needed to satisfy an urge for revenge upon those who had taken the lives of his brothers. He enlisted at Philadelphia at age twenty-six for a period of one year and was listed as having a dark complexion, hazel eyes, black hair, and standing at about 5'5" in height. As his regiment took the field near Petersburg, Virginia, the Tubbs family received the shocking news that Elias had died at the hospital at City Point on October 28 due to an infection of his wound, along with severe diarrhea.

Daniel, the only remaining brother, accompanied his regiment into winter quarters with the rest of the XXIV Corps. There the 199th learned the art of soldiering, being drilled each day to prepare for the upcoming campaign in 1865. The end of the war was now in sight, as Lee's forces were bottled up in and around the City of Petersburg, Virginia. Grant's army settled down for a long winter in front of the besieged city. Daniel was admitted to the hospital in January for an unknown illness, but was back with his comrades by February. By March of 1865, time was running out for the Confederate army, and Lieutenant General Grant issued marching orders for his army. The 199th, along with the other regiments of the division, was ordered to attack strong enemy fortifications at Fort Gregg. On April 2, the 199th regiment bravely attacked the fort. It was initially forced to fall back to its original position due to a lack of reinforcements, but it reformed and attacked several more times before the fort was ultimately captured. During one of these assaults, Private Daniel Tubbs was shot in the chest by an enemy musket ball.

Daniel was immediately removed from the field and sent to Fortress Monroe hospital to recover. During the Civil War, any torso wound was particularly dangerous, as medicine of the period was primitive at best. The risk of infection was great, and since there were no antibiotics, physicians were virtually helpless to actively prevent or treat them, especially with regard to a chest wound. Infections in an extremity could be eliminated by amputating that extremity, but that was not an option with a torso wound. Daniel remained at the hospital until May 15, when he was discharged from the army to return home.

He had lived to see the end of the war, but his wound would not allow him to live more than a month after he returned home to his wife, children, and parents. He died of infection and chronic diarrhea on June 19, 1865 at his home in Salem Township with his family at his side. The last of the brothers was gone.

The effects of the Civil War were devastating for the Tubbs family. Not only did Rebecca and Earl lose their four sons, but also three women lost their husbands, and four children lost their fathers. The generation that fought for the Union in those terrible years paid a high price. The remains of Josiah Tubbs lie at the Andersonville Cemetery in grave number 6,447, alongside thousands of others who gave all for the Union. It is believed that the remains of Elias, Joseph, and Daniel lie near the stone pictured in this book at the Scott Cemetery in Huntington Mills. However, it is very possible that Joseph and Elias are buried near where they died at Bethesda Church and City Point, Virginia, respectively.

Rebecca received a pension of $8 per month for the death of Joseph and each wife received a pension for the death of her husband. The surviving children of each man also received a payment of $10 per month until they reached the age of sixteen. Interestingly, it was discovered that Felicianna, the widow of Daniel, remarried a man named Henry W. Moore in 1868. The couple, along with the children of Daniel, moved to Berwick. In June of 1875, Moore left his home and was never heard from again, whereupon which time, Felicianna applied for a widow's pension once again.

PRIVATE JOSEPH P. TUBBS?, CO. K, 7TH PENNSYLVANIA RESERVES – PHOTO IS IDENTIFIED AS "J.P. TUBBS" UNIT UNKNOWN –
IT IS STRONGLY SUSPECTED THAT HE IS INDEED JOSEPH TUBBS.
CREDIT: U.S. ARMY MILITARY HISTORY INSTITUTE COLLECTION

Gone But Not Forgotten | *Civil War Veterans of Northeastern Pennsylvania*

JOSIAH, DANIEL, ELIAS, AND JOSEPH TUBBS, ALL BROTHERS, DIED DURING THE COURSE OF THE WAR.
SCOTT CEMETERY, HUNTINGTON MILLS
CREDIT: RYAN LINDBUCHLER PHOTO

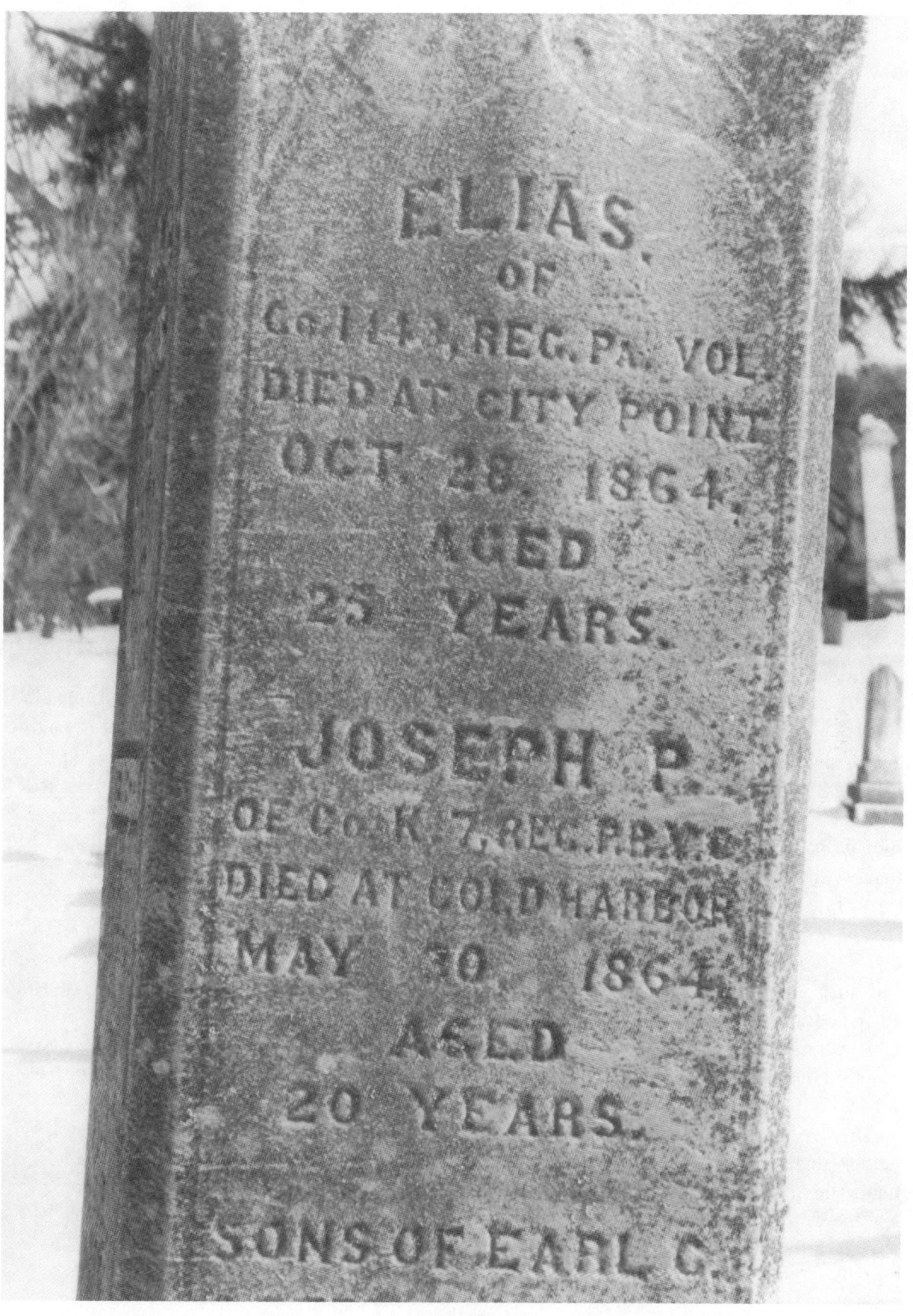

David M. Jones
1839 – October 25, 1896

The year 1864 had been a bloody one for the Union. The newly appointed general-in-chief, Ulysses S. Grant, had lost over 60,000 men through the spring and summer of that year. The people of the north were tired of war, but knew that Grant would not back down against Lee's Army of Northern Virginia, as other Union generals had done. Even though Grant was called "the butcher" by many in the north, the fighting men of the Union army had faith and confidence in him. By late summer the Union army had settled down to a siege of the city of Petersburg, Virginia, just south of the Confederate capital at Richmond.

The Commonwealth of Pennsylvania was in the process of raising regiments to serve for a period of one year, in order to replenish Grant's thinned ranks. One such regiment was the 199th Pennsylvania Volunteer Infantry. Three companies would be partially made up of Luzerne County men. On September 19, Company I ("Alleman Fencibles") was being raised at Scranton and many men took the oath to protect the Union at all costs. One of these men was Corporal David M. Jones. The 5'4", blue eyed, light haired man was from Scranton and perhaps wished to see a bit of the war firsthand. The twenty-five year old was a moulder by trade, and at one time worked in one of the many coal mines of northeastern Pennsylvania. Records indicate that he was born in South Wales in 1839 and was married to a woman named Hannah at the time of his enlistment.

The newly formed company was joined with the rest of the regiment and then proceeded to the front in October. It was assigned to the Army of the James in its XXIV Corps, and performed fortification duties at Deep Bottom Landing. The regiment's first taste of army life was not using a rifle, but using a shovel. The regiment proceeded to build fortifications, roads, bridges, and whatever else was necessary to strengthen the position of the brigade. Jones was promoted to corporal on October 2, and the regiment spent winter quarters learning the art of soldiering. It was ready to engage the enemy in the spring of 1865.

On April 2, the regiment was ordered to attack a Confederate fortification along the Petersburg defenses called Fort Gregg. The men attacked ferociously and acted more like veterans of a hundred battles, rather than veterans of none. By the end of the day, the fort had been taken and the Confederates manning the fort were driven out with two-thirds lying dead or wounded. However, the 199th regiment suffered greatly, as it lost 109 men in the attack. Company I lost one of its lieutenants, its first sergeant, and one corporal. The corporal's name was David M.

Jones. While charging the position, a Confederate minié ball struck his right shin, shattering the bones that were within. Jones fell to the ground, feeling that peculiar burning sensation, near the wound, that one feels when shot. He was able to drag himself back toward the Union position and was picked up after the battle by ambulance personnel.

Medical procedures of the period were very primitive when compared to today's methods. Medical technology that we take for granted today did not exist during the 1860s. As a result, there was no way to repair a shattered limb. Simple ideas about sanitation and sterility did not exist, and an open wound created a safe harbor for infection that could cause gangrene and consequently death if the limb was not removed by amputation. At a nearby field hospital, Jones' right leg was amputated above the knee, making him an invalid for the rest of his life.

Jones was sent to David's Island, New York, to rest and recuperate from his wound. He was discharged on October 3, 1865, from the hospital. He returned home to his wife Hannah in Scranton. He was awarded a pension of $8 per month in 1865. Obviously, heavy physical labor was out of the question, so Jones worked at various clerical jobs to supplement his income. In 1870, Hannah died of unknown causes. Three years later, he would meet and marry a local woman named Annie E. Williams. The couple was married in Plymouth, Pennsylvania, on September 23, 1873. In December of 1881 Annie would give birth to a daughter they named Helen. Helen was the first of three children, as Dora would be born in 1883 and Ethel in 1886.

In 1874, Jones was receiving a $24 per month pension, and applied to the government to have that rate increased because his wound was causing him to put much strain on his heart while getting around. Jones' doctor submitted a letter to the pension bureau stating that the strain of getting around made it impossible to perform any kind of work. The request was turned down as the government determined that the wound was not responsible for any heart condition that Jones may have had.

In 1896, the government received a notice by Doctor W.G. Allen, the Jones' family physician. It read: "David Jones died on October the 25 as a result of hypertrophy of the heart, which was a result of having lost his right leg and thigh while in the service." He went further to state that Jones had Bright's Disease (a disease of the kidneys) as a result of his amputation. He was laid to rest at the Washburn Street Cemetery in Scranton and was joined by his wife Annie some years later.

Gone But Not Forgotten | *Civil War Veterans of Northeastern Pennsylvania*

CORPORAL DAVID M. JONES, CO. I, 199TH PENNSYLVANIA VOLUNTEER INFANTRY
CREDIT: G.A.R. POST 139 COLLECTION

MERRITT SLOCUM HARDING
October 20, 1839 – April 7, 1906

In the spring of 1861, war fever was consuming the nation. The surrender of U.S. forces at Fort Sumter may have been far away from Factoryville, Pennsylvania, but one would not know it by the patriotism shown by the men of this town. In April, 1861, local men there began recruiting a company to serve the Commonwealth in crushing the rebellion. The group became known as the "Factoryville Infantry" and would serve as Company B of the 12th Pennsylvania Reserve Infantry Regiment.

A twenty-one year-old farmer from Plains (Plainsville), Pennsylvania, joined their ranks, promising to protect the Union as a soldier for a period of three years or the duration of the war. Many thought the war would last only a few short months, and perhaps Merritt S. Harding was of this opinion. Immediately, his comrades elected the blue-eyed, dark haired farmer-turned-soldier to the rank of corporal. At the commencement of the war, this method of promotion was common among volunteer regiments.

The men were initially moved to Harrisburg, where they were mustered into service on May 15, 1861. The regiment was attached to the Pennsylvania Reserve Corps and received training at Camp Curtin (named after Governor Andrew G. Curtin). The 12th did not take part in the Union debacle at Bull Run in July, but was sent to the front in August, where it was attached to the third brigade, with the many other Reserve Infantry Regiments. Near Washington, the 12th received more training as soldiers, and first engaged the enemy at Drainesville, Virginia, on December 20, losing only one man. Harding spent the winter in quarters with the rest of his company near Washington until it took the field once again in March, 1862.

In May and June of 1862, the 12th was engaged several times in battle with the enemy and lost heavily at New Market Crossroads in June. Harding bravely fought with his company and was recognized as a good soldier when he was selected to serve in the color-company of the regiment. To be chosen for this duty was very prestigious, as only the best and bravest of any regiment were chosen to bear and protect the colors (flags) of the regiment. Harding was chosen to carry the regimental colors, one of only two flags held by the 12th, and managed to survive unscathed through the month of July. Arguably, the position of color bearer was the most dangerous post in any Civil War regiment. This is because the enemy would most likely fire at the regimental color bearers in an attempt to confuse and demoralize the opposing force. It was not uncommon for a regiment to have several color bearers killed or wounded in one engagement.

Harding carried the colors into battle on August 29, as Union forces engaged the enemy at Manassas, Virginia. Just one-year earlier, Union forces had been defeated by the Confederate army there, ending all hope that it would be a short war. In the blistering sun, the 12th Reserves went into battle near Henry House Hill and immediately came under artillery fire and later small arms fire, losing many men in the process. The next day, the regiment (along with the rest of the brigade) was ordered to a position on Henry House Hill where the brigade made a daring charge upon the enemy. It is believed that during this charge Corporal Harding was violently thrown to the ground, struck by two enemy musket balls. The first one entered his right hand above the knuckle of his pinkie finger and traveled through his hand, exiting his body at the wrist, resulting in a hideous wound. The second went through his right shoulder, luckily not damaging any major organs or blood vessels. Harding managed to carry the colors from the field, passing them to Lieutenant Edward Kelly of Company E when he became weak from loss of blood.

Harding was eventually sent to Carver Hospital in Washington, D.C., where bones were removed from his wrist in an attempt to prevent infection. Harding spent the next six months at Carver recuperating from his wounds. In March, 1863, he was discharged from the 12th for disability and returned home to Plains a battle worn veteran. Little is known about his life immediately following his discharge, but it is known for certain that he was married to Martha S. Kishbaugh on September 11, 1864. The couple was married in Eaton Township, Wyoming County, where it is presumed the bride lived before the marriage.

The young couple separated only six days later when Harding accepted a commission as second lieutenant of Company C, 127th United States Colored Troops. Since 1863, the federal government had accepted African-Americans into the army to serve in segregated regiments. Regulations stated that blacks could not serve as commissioned officers, so this duty fell to qualified white officers. This was a particularly hazardous duty because the Confederate government had issued orders to its army to execute any white officers captured while commanding black troops. Nevertheless, Harding served as an officer in Company C, earning a promotion to first lieutenant.

The 127th was organized in late summer of 1864 and was attached to the Army of the James, where it was engaged in battle at Deep Bottom, Virginia, in the fall of the same year. Soon after, the 127th was sent south to serve in Texas on the Mexican frontier and was later consolidated into three companies. Harding was discharged in October, 1865, five months after the close of the war in the West, and returned home to his wife where the couple resided in Plains. They soon had their first daughter, Letta, in 1867, and would have seven more children in the next fifteen years. In April, 1906, the grizzled veteran of many battles, and heroic color-bearer of the 12th Pennsylvania Reserves, died at his home in Plains. His remains lie in the Hollenback Cemetery close to several hundred comrades who served in the war to preserve the Union.

Lieutenant Merritt S. Harding, 12th Pennsylvania Reserves & 127th U.S. Colored Troops,
Hollenback Cemetery, Wilkes-Barre
Credit: Kristen Lindbuchler Photo

Gone But Not Forgotten | *Civil War Veterans of Northeastern Pennsylvania*

G.A.R. Memorial - Catawissa, Pennsylvania
Credit: Ryan Lindbuchler photo

Ryan Lindbuchler

G.A.R. MEMORIAL - FREELAND, PENNSYLVANIA
CREDIT: KRISTEN LINDBUCHLER PHOTO

Gone But Not Forgotten | *Civil War Veterans of Northeastern Pennsylvania*

G.A.R. Memorial - Hollenback Cemetery, Wilkes-Barre, Pennsylvania
Credit: Kristen Lindbuchler photo

Civil War Section - Cathedral Cemetery, Scranton, Pennsylvania
Credit: Ryan Lindbuchler photo

Gone But Not Forgotten | *Civil War Veterans of Northeastern Pennsylvania*

Civil War Section - Shawnee Cemetery, Plymouth, Pennsylvania

Ryan Lindbuchler

G.A.R. Memorial - Oddfellow's Cemetery, Tamaqua, Pennsylvania
Credit: Ryan Lindbuchler photo

Gone But Not Forgotten | *Civil War Veterans of Northeastern Pennsylvania*

Memorial to Private William L. Millham, Co. A, 52nd Pennsylvania Volunteer Infantry
Wilkes-Barre City Cemetery
Credit: Kristen Lindbuchler photo

Unknown Soldier - Wyoming Cemetery
Credit: Ryan Lindbuchler photo

Regimental Sketches

The following list is made up of regiments and/or companies that were composed of men from northeastern and central Pennsylvania. The regimental sketches that follow this list are intended to give the reader knowledge of regimental activities during the war, and to give the number of graves located throughout the area.

INFANTRY REGIMENTS

8th Pennsylvania Volunteer Infantry Regiment

11th Pennsylvania Volunteer Infantry Regiment

15th Pennsylvania Volunteer Infantry Regiment

28th Pennsylvania Volunteer Infantry Regiment

48th Pennsylvania Volunteer Infantry Regiment

52nd Pennsylvania Volunteer Infantry Regiment

Company F, 53rd Pennsylvania Volunteer Infantry Regiment

Company D, 61st Pennsylvania Volunteer Infantry Regiment

81st Pennsylvania Volunteer Infantry Regiment

96th Pennsylvania Volunteer Infantry Regiment

104th Pennsylvania Volunteer Infantry Regiment

132nd Pennsylvania Volunteer Infantry Regiment

143rd Pennsylvania Volunteer Infantry Regiment

147th Pennsylvania Volunteer Infantry Regiment

Company F, 149th Pennsylvania Volunteer Infantry Regiment

199th Pennsylvania Volunteer Infantry Regiment

203rd Pennsylvania Volunteer Infantry Regiment

INFANTRY RESERVE REGIMENTS

Company A, 6th RESERVES (35th regiment of the line)
Company F, 7th RESERVES (36th regiment of the line)

CAVALRY REGIMENTS

4th Pennsylvania Volunteer Cavalry Regiment
(64th regiment of the line)

9th Pennsylvania Volunteer Cavalry Regiment
(92nd regiment of the line)

17th Pennsylvania Volunteer Cavalry Regiment
(162nd regiment of the line)

ARTILLERY REGIMENTS

1st Pennsylvania Volunteer Light Artillery Regiment
(43rd regiment of the line)

2nd Pennsylvania Volunteer Heavy Artillery Regiment
(112th regiment of the line)

3rd Pennsylvania Volunteer Heavy Artillery Regiment
(152nd regiment of the line)

8TH PENNSYLVANIA VOLUNTEER INFANTRY REGIMENT

Organized: April, 1861

Companies: A – Northumberland County / B-H – **Luzerne** County / I, K – Jefferson County

Company Nicknames:
- A – Shamokin Guards
- B – Covington Fencibles
- C – Wyoming Light Dragoons
- D – Jackson Rifles
- E – Luzerne Guard
- F – Wyoming Artillerists
- G – Wyoming Jaeger Rifles
- H – Scranton Union Vols.
- I – Brookville Rifles
- K – Brookville Rifles

Corps: General Patterson's Corps   **Division:** First   **Brigade:** Third

Battles: This ninety-day regiment was composed mostly of militiamen from northeastern Pennsylvania and was placed under the command of General Robert Patterson in May of 1861. Patterson was charged with capturing the Federal arsenal at Harper's Ferry, which had been taken by Confederate troops under Confederate General Thomas J. Jackson. Patterson was also charged with the responsibility of preventing Confederate troops from evacuating western Virginia to reinforce Confederate forces in eastern Virginia about to fight the first Battle of Bull Run.

Unfortunately, Patterson was unable to complete his mission, and Jackson's men slipped away to join Beauregard's troops at Manassas, resulting in a Confederate victory. Harper's Ferry was taken by Patterson's men only after it had been abandoned. The 8th was only lightly engaged in skirmishes with the enemy and was mustered out eight days after the Union defeat at Bull Run. Many men who had served in the 8th would later join three year regiments, especially the 143rd Pennsylvania Volunteer Infantry.

Most Destructive Battle: none

Mustered Out of Service: July 29, 1861

Largest Concentration of Graves: 19 at Cathedral Cemetery, Scranton, Pennsylvania - Lackawanna County (Luzerne County during the Civil War)

Number of Graves Located: 105

11th Pennsylvania Volunteer Infantry Regiment

Organized: August, 1861

Companies: A – Cumberland and Dauphin Counties / B – Clinton County
C – Westmoreland County / D – Lycoming and Northumberland Counties / E – Westmoreland, Northumberland, and Lancaster Counties / F – Westmoreland County / G – Allegheny County
H – **Carbon** County / I – Westmoreland County / K – Westmoreland County

Company Nicknames:
A – Sumner Rifles   F – Salem Union Guards

Corps: First   **Division:** Second   **Brigade:** Third
Fifth   Third   Second

Battles: Thoroughfare Gap, Second Bull Run, Antietam, Fredericksburg, Gettysburg, Wilderness, North Anna, Cold Harbor, Spotsylvania Court House, Petersburg, Weldon Railroad, Hatcher's Run, Gravelly Run, and Five Forks.

Most Destructive Battle: Gettysburg (July 1, 1863). The regiment lost about 140 out of about 212 engaged.

Mustered Out of Service: July 1, 1865

Largest Concentration of Graves: 14 at the Grand Army Cemetery, Summit Hill, Pennsylvania.

Number of Graves Located: 41 men of Company H

15ᵀᴴ Pennsylvania Volunteer Infantry Regiment

Organized: May, 1861

Companies: A-D – **Luzerne** County / E – Dauphin County / F – Lancaster County
G – **Luzerne** County / H – Huntingdon County / I – Centre County / K – Lancaster County

Company Nicknames:

A – Keystone Guards	B – White Haven Jaegers	C – Lackawanna Rifles
D – Pittston Artillery	E – Verbeke Rifles	F – Washington Rifles
G – Nagle Light Infantry	H – Union Guards	I – Curtin Infantry
K – Marietta Cameron Guards		

Corps: General Patterson's Corps   **Division:** Second   **Brigade:** Fifth

Battles: This ninety-day regiment saw little action with the exception of an action that took place when men of the 15th were engaged by a Confederate force under Colonel Turner Ashby on July 2, 1861. Company I of the 15th, along with a company from the 14th P.V.I., were sent out ahead of the main force as skirmishers to locate the position of the enemy. Ashby's men, wearing Union blue blouses, captured thirty four men.

Mustered Out of Service: August 7, 1861

Largest Concentration of Graves: 11 at the Laurel Cemetery, White Haven, Pennsylvania – Luzerne County

Number of Graves Located: 68

28ᵀᴴ Pennsylvania Volunteer Infantry Regiment

Organized: June, 1861

Companies: A – **Luzerne** County / B – Westmoreland County / C, D – Philadelphia
E – **Carbon** County / F-H – Allegheny County / I, K – Philadelphia / L – Allegheny County and Philadelphia / M – Philadelphia / N – **Luzerne** County / O – Huntingdon County
P – Philadelphia

Company Nicknames:
A – Pardee Guards C – Geary Guards D – 2ⁿᵈ Co. Indep. Grays
E – Mauch Chunk Rangers F – Elizabeth Mountaineers G – Sewickley Rifles
H – Zouave Cadets L – McKnight Guards M – Union Grays
O – Lawrence Rifles P – Scott Legion

* Companies L, M, N, O, and P were transferred to the 147ᵗʰ Penna. Volunteer Infantry in October of 1862.

Corps: Twelfth   **Division:** Second   **Brigade:** First

Battles: Linden, Cedar Creek, Antietam, Chancellorsville, Gettysburg, Wauhatchie, Ringgold, Rocky Face Ridge, New Hope Church, Pine Knob, Culp's Farm, Lookout Mountain, Resaca, Kenesaw Mountain, Marietta, Peach Tree Creek, Dalton, Atlanta, Savannah, and Port Edisto.

Most Destructive Battle: Antietam (September 17, 1862). The regiment lost 266 men. According to Samuel Bates, the regiment captured two enemy artillery pieces and five regimental flags in its fierce fight near the Dunker Church.

Mustered Out of Service: July 18, 1865

Largest Concentration of Graves: 30 at the Vine Street Cemetery, Hazleton –
                                    Luzerne County

Number of Graves Located: 164

48ᵀᴴ Pennsylvania Volunteer Infantry Regiment

Organized: September, 1861

Companies: A-K – Schuylkill County

Company Nicknames:
A – Port Clinton Artillery B – Haskin Guards C – Tower Guards
D – Nagle Guards E – Wynkoop Artillerists F – Ringgold Rifles
G – Washington Artillery H – Scott Infantry I – Anthracite Infantry
K – Wilder Guards

Corps: Ninth   **Division:** Second   **Brigade:** First

Battles: New Berne, N.C., Chantilly, Second Bull Run, South Mountain, Antietam, Fredericksburg, Campbell's Station, Knoxville, Blue Springs, Wilderness, Spotsylvania, North Anna, Bethesda Church, Cold Harbor, Petersburg, Peebles' Farm, Weldon Railroad, Hatcher's Run.

* The 48ᵗʰ is most famous for constructing a mine during the siege of Petersburg, Virginia in late 1864. Most of the men in the regiment had been coal miners as civilians and were proficient at constructing mine shafts. Because of this knowledge, Lieutenant Colonel Pleasants proposed the idea that his regiment, the 48ᵗʰ, construct a mine shaft over five hundred feet long under the Confederate fortifications. The idea was approved and the regiment constructed the tunnel, placing 8,000 pounds of gunpowder under the Confederate line. The powder was exploded, allowing Union forces to pour through the breach, known afterwards as the "Crater". The attack was ultimately unsuccessful, but the accomplishments of the regiment were praised by the U.S. general staff.

Most Destructive Battle: Spotsylvania (May 12, 1864). The regiment lost 103 men.

Mustered Out of Service: July 17, 1865

Largest Concentration of Graves: 49 at Charles Baber Cemetery, Pottsville, Pennsylvania – Schuykill County

Number of Graves Located: 294

52ⁿᴰ Pennsylvania Volunteer Infantry Regiment
"The Luzerne Regiment"

Organized: October, 1861

Companies: A – **Luzerne** County / B – Wyoming County / C – Clinton County
D – Union and Snyder Counties / E, F – Bradford County / G – Columbia County
H, I, K – **Luzerne** and Schuylkill Counties

Company Nicknames:
A – Mayer Rifles	B – Wyoming Rangers	C – Mackey Guards
E – Mountain Lake Rangers	G – Keystone Sharpshooters	K – Fellows Guards

Corps: Fourth **Division:** Third **Brigade:** First

Battles: Yorktown, Fair Oaks, Seven Pines, and Fort Johnson.

* According to Bates' *History of Pennsylvania Volunteers*, the regiment's state flag was the first U.S. flag to be flown over Fort Sumter since its surrender in April of 1861. The regiment's flag flew over Sumter's ruins on February 18, 1865.

Most Destructive Battle: Fair Oaks (May 30, 1862). The regiment lost 125 out of 249 engaged.

Mustered Out of Service: July 12, 1865

Largest Concentration of Graves: 31 at the Dunmore Cemetery, Dunmore, Pennsylvania – Lackawanna County (Luzerne County during the Civil War).

Number of Graves Located: 340

53RD PENNSYLVANIA VOLUNTEER INFANTRY REGIMENT

Organized: September, 1861

Companies: A, B – Montgomery County / C – Blair and Huntingdon Counties
D – Centre and Clearfield Counties / E – **Carbon** and Union Counties
F – **Luzerne County** / G – Potter County / H – Northumberland and Montour Counties
I – Juniata County / K – Westmoreland County

Company Nicknames:
A – Madison Guards   B – Downingtown Guards   C – James Creek Guards
D – McCann Rifles   E – Rooke Guards   F – Wyoming Guards
G – Jones Rifles   H – Lawson Guards   I – Union Guards
K – Latrobe Light Guards

Corps: Second   **Division:** First   **Brigade:** Fourth

Battles: Fair Oaks, Antietam, Fredericksburg, Chancellorsville, Gettysburg, Bristoe Station, Mine Run, Wilderness, Spotsylvania, North Anna, Cold Harbor, Petersburg, Deep Bottom, Reams' Station, White Oak Road, Five Forks, Strawberry Plains, Farmville, and Appomattox.

Most Destructive Battle: Spotsylvania (May 12, 1864). The regiment lost 177 men.

Mustered Out of Service: June 30, 1865

Largest Concentration of Graves: 5 at the Fern Knoll Cemetery, Dallas, Pennsylvania – Luzerne County

Number of Company F Graves Located: 54

61ST PENNSYLVANIA VOLUNTEER INFANTRY REGIMENT

Organized: August, 1861

Companies: A – Indiana County / B, C – Allegheny County / D – **Luzerne** County
E, F – Allegheny County / G, H, I – Philadelphia / K – Allegheny County

Company Nicknames:
A – Mahoning Rifle Guards   B – Ellsworth Legion   C – Richard Guards
D – Emley Zouaves   E – Simpson Light Infantry   F – Allegheny Guards
G – Holt Guards   H – Independent Greys   K – 1st Penna. Zouaves

Corps: Fourth   **Division:** First   **Brigade:** First
  Sixth   Second   Third

Battles: Yorktown, Fair Oaks, Malvern Hill, Antietam, Salem Heights, Williamsport, Fredericksburg, Gettysburg, Marye's Heights (1863), Rappahannock Station, Wilderness, Spotsylvania, Cold Harbor, Fort Stevens, Charlestown, Opequon, Fisher's Hill, Cedar Creek, Petersburg, Sailor's Creek, and Appomattox.

Most Destructive Battle: Fair Oaks (May 31, 1862). According to Fox's _Regimental Losses in the Civil War_, the 61st suffered more casualties than any other Federal regiment in that battle: 263 men were lost that day.

Mustered Out of Service: June 28, 1865

Largest Concentration of Graves: 10 at the Hollenback Cemetery, Wilkes-Barre, Pennsylvania– Luzerne County

Number of Company D Graves Located: 40

Medal of Honor Winner
<u>Captain (then Sergeant) Sylvester D. Rhodes</u> - *of Company D, was awarded the Medal of Honor for leading his company at the Battle of Fisher's Hill on September 22, 1864. Rhodes' men assaulted a Confederate position and captured two artillery pieces, turning the guns on retreating Confederate troops. Rhodes' grave is located at the Hollenback Cemetery in Wilkes-Barre, Pennsylvania.*

81ST PENNSYLVANIA VOLUNTEER INFANTRY REGIMENT
"THE CHIPPEWA REGIMENT"

Organized: October, 1861

Companies: A-F - Philadephia / G, H, I - Carbon County / K - **Luzerne** and **Carbon** Counties

Company Nicknames:
F – 2nd Company, Cadwalader Greys   K – Council Ridge Rifles

Corps: Second   **Division:** First   **Brigade:** First

Battles: Fair Oaks, Yorktown, Savage Station, White Oak Swamp, Glendale, Malvern Hill, Antietam, Fredericksburg, Chancellorsville, Gettysburg, Bristoe Station, Mine Run, Wilderness, Spotsylvania, Po River, Totopotomoy, North Anna, Cold Harbor, Petersburg, Deep Bottom, Strawberry Plains, Ream's Station, Hatcher's Run, Farmville, and Appomattox.

Most Destructive Battle: Fredericksburg (December 13, 1862). The regiment lost 176 out of 261 engaged.

Mustered Out of Service: June 29, 1865

Largest Concentration of Graves: 23 at the Union Cemetery, Weatherly, Pennsylvania – Carbon County

Number of Graves Located: 204

96th Pennsylvania Volunteer Infantry Regiment

Organized: September, 1861

Companies: A-D – Schuylkill County / E – **Luzerne** and Schuylkill Counties
F – Schuylkill County / G – Schuylkill, Berks, and Dauphin Counties
H-K – Schuylkill County.

Company Nicknames:
A – National Light Infantry
B – Pine Grove Sharpshooters
C – Good Intent Light Artillery
F – Union Guards
G – Hamburg Light Infantry

Corps: Sixth   **Division:** First   **Brigade:** First

Battles: Seven Days, Gaines' Mill, Crampton's Gap, Antietam, Fredericksburg, Bowling Green Road, Salem Heights, Marye's Heights (1863), Gettysburg, Wilderness, Spotsylvania, Cedar Creek, Cold Harbor, Petersburg, Opequon, and Fisher's Hill.

Most Destructive Battle: Spotsylvania (May 10, 1864). The regiment lost 178 men out of about 350 engaged.

Mustered Out of Service: September 22, 1864

Largest Concentration of Graves: 27 at Charles Baber Cemetery, Pottsville, Pennsylvania - Schuylkill County

Number of Graves Located: 141

104TH PENNSYLVANIA VOLUNTEER INFANTRY REGIMENT

Organized: August, 1861

Companies: A-D – Bucks County / E – Bucks and Blair Counties / F – Bucks and Perry Counties / G – Bucks and Schuylkill Counties / H – Berks County / I – Philadelphia, Bucks and **Luzerne** Counties / K – Bucks, Armstrong, and Allegheny Counties

Company Nicknames:
A – Young Guard   B – Old Guard   C – McClellan Rangers
H – Lauer Infantry

Corps: Fourth   **Division:** Third   **Brigade:** First

Battles: Yorktown, Savage's Station, Fair Oaks, Siege of Charleston, Siege of Fort Wagner, Cedar Creek, and Petersburg.

Most Destructive Battle: Fair Oaks (May 31, 1862). The regiment lost 237 men.

Mustered Out of Service: August 25, 1865

Largest Concentration of Graves: 20 at the Odd Fellows' Cemetery, Tamaqua, Pennsylvania – Schuylkill County

Number of Graves Located: 106

Medal of Honor Winner:
<u>Sergeant Hiram Pursell</u> - Company G, was awarded the Medal of Honor for rescuing the regiment's colors at the Battle of Fair Oaks. He is interred at the Laurel Cemetery, White Haven, Pennsylvania (Luzerne County). Rendition of this event painted by William Trego in 1899 appears as the cover of this book.

132ND PENNSYLVANIA VOLUNTEER INFANTRY REGIMENT

Organized: August, 1862

Companies: A – Montour County / B – Wyoming County / C, D – Bradford County
E – Columbia County / F, G – **Carbon** County / H – Columbia County
I, K – **Luzerne** County

Company Nicknames:
A – Danville Fencibles   B – Wyoming Tigers   E – Bloomsburg Guards
F - Lehigh Valley Guards   H – Catawissa Guards   I – Railroad Guards
K – Scranton Guards

Corps: Second   **Division:** Third   **Brigade:** Third

Battles: South Mountain, Antietam, Fredericksburg, Chancellorsville

Most Destructive Battle: Antietam (September 17, 1862). The regiment lost 152 men out of 492 engaged.

Mustered Out of Service: May 24, 1863

Largest Concentration of Graves: 16 at the Evergreen Cemetery, Factoryville, Pennsylvania – Wyoming County

Number of Graves Located: 204

143RD PENNSYLVANIA VOLUNTEER INFANTRY REGIMENT

Organized: October, 1862

Companies: A-G – **Luzerne** County / H – Susquehanna County / I – **Luzerne** County
K – Lycoming and Wyoming Counties

Company Nicknames:
A – Ross Rifles   C – Wyoming Artillerists   D – Wyoming Light Dragoons

Corps: First   **Division:** Third   **Brigade:** Second
         Fifth   Fourth   First

Battles: Chancellorsville, Gettysburg, Wilderness, Laurel Hill, Spotsylvania, North Anna, Cold Harbor, Totopotomoy, Petersburg, Weldon Railroad, Bethesda Church, Boydton Road, and Hatcher's Run.

Most Destructive Battle: The Wilderness (May 3, 1864). The regiment lost 220 out of about 450 men engaged.

Mustered Out of Service: June 12, 1865

Largest Concentration of Graves: 40 at the Hollenback Cemetery, Wilkes-Barre – Luzerne County

Number of Graves Located: 392

Medal of Honor Winners Located:

<u>Sergeant James M. Rutter</u> – Company C, Hollenback Cemetery, Wilkes-Barre, Pennsylvania. Was awarded the Medal of Honor for gallantry at the Battle of Gettysburg on July 1, 1863.

<u>Lieutenant (then Sergeant) Patrick DeLacy</u> – Company A, Moscow Cemetery, Moscow, Pennsylvania. Was awarded the Medal of Honor for gallantry at the Battle of the Wilderness on May 6, 1864.

147ᵀᴴ Pennsylvania Volunteer Infantry Regiment

Organized: October, 1862

Companies: A – Allegheny County / B – Huntingdon County, Philadelphia
C – **Luzerne** County / D – Philadelphia / E – Philadelphia / F – **Luzerne** County
G – Snyder County / H – Lehigh and Berks Counties / I – Philadelphia and Berks Counties
K – **Carbon** County

Company Nicknames:
A – Old Company L, 28ᵗʰ P.V.I.   B – Old Company O, 28ᵗʰ P.V.I.
C – Old Company N, 28ᵗʰ P.V.I.   D – Old Company M, 28ᵗʰ P.V.I.
E – Old Company P, 28ᵗʰ P.V.I.   G – Keystone Guards
I – Schuylkill Arsenal Guard

** Note: the regiment was raised from five extra companies that the 28ᵗʰ Pennsylvania Volunteer Infantry Regiment had in its ranks. The 147ᵗʰ was supplemented with five more companies of recruits to make the mandatory ten that were needed to fill the ranks. The 147ᵗʰ and the 28ᵗʰ were brigaded together in the XII Corps.

Corps: Twelfth   **Division:** Second   **Brigade:** First
     Twentieth   Second   First

Battles: Chancellorsville, Gettysburg, Lookout Mountain, Ringgold, New Hope Church,
    Pine Knob, Kenesaw Mountain, Peach Tree Creek, Atlanta, and Savannah.

Most Destructive Battle: Chancellorsville (May 3, 1863). The regiment lost 94 out of about
    500 men engaged.

Mustered Out of Service: July 15, 1865

Largest Concentration of Graves: 37 at the Vine Street Cemetery, Hazleton, Pennsylvania –
    Luzerne County.

Number of Graves Located: 108

149TH PENNSYLVANIA VOLUNTEER INFANTRY REGIMENT

Organized: August, 1862

Companies: A – Tioga County / B – Clearfield County / C – Lebanon County
D – Allegheny County / E – Clearfield and **Luzerne** Counties / F – **Luzerne** County
G – Potter, Tioga, and Perry Counties / H – Mifflin County / I – Huntingdon County
K – Potter County

Company Nicknames:
C – Jackson Guards   F – Huntingdon Valley Rifles

Corps:	First	**Division:**	Third	**Brigade:**	Second
	Fifth		First		First
	Fifth		Third		First

Battles: Chancellorsville, Gettysburg, Wilderness, Spotsylvania, North Anna, Bethesda Church, Cold Harbor, Petersburg, Totopotomoy, Weldon Railroad, Peeble's Farm, Hatcher's Run, and Dabney's Mills.

Most Destructive Battle: Gettysburg (July 1, 1863). The regiment lost 336 of 450 men engaged.

Mustered Out of Service: June 24, 1865

Largest Concentration of Graves: 6 at Dodson Cemetery, Town Hill, Pennsylvania – Luzerne County.

Number of Company F Graves Located: 45

199TH PENNSYLVANIA VOLUNTEER INFANTRY REGIMENT
"THE COMMERCIAL REGIMENT"

Organized: September, 1864

Companies: A – Philadelphia and Montgomery County / B – Philadelphia
C – **Luzerne** County and Philadelphia / D,E – Philadelphia / F – Crawford County
G – Philadelphia, **Luzerne** and Lancaster Counties / H – Philadelphia, Erie, Fayette, and Allegheny Counties / I- **Luzerne** and Lycoming Counties / K – Lancaster and Erie Counties

Company Nicknames:
I – Alleman Fencibles

Corps: Twenty-fourth   **Division:** First   **Brigade:** First

Battles: Petersburg (Forts Gregg and Alexander), Rice's Station, and Appomattox.

Most Destructive Battle: Petersburg (April 2, 1865). The regiment lost 109 men in the assault on Forts Gregg and Alexander.

Mustered Out of Service: June 28, 1865

Largest Concentration of Graves: 15 at the Pine Hill Cemetery, Shickshinny, Pennsylvania – Luzerne County.

Number of Graves Located: 123

203ʳᵈ Pennsylvania Volunteer Infantry Regiment
"Birney's Sharpshooters"

Organized: September, 1864

Companies: A – Lancaster County / B – Chester and Delaware Counties
C – **Luzerne** and Susquehanna Counties / D – Philadelphia, Chester and **Luzerne** Counties
E, F – Lancaster and **Luzerne** Counties / G – Lycoming, Clinton, and Centre Counties
H – Lancaster County / I – Lycoming County / K – **Luzerne** and Lancaster Counties

Company Nicknames:
A – Lancaster Sharpshooters

Corps: Tenth   **Division:** Second   **Brigade:** Second
Twenty fourth   Second   Second

Battles: Deep Bottom, Chapin's Farm, Petersburg, Fort Fisher, Wilmington, and Raleigh.

Most Destructive Battle: Fort Fisher (January 2, 1865). The regiment lost 191 out of about 450 engaged.

Mustered Out of Service: June 22, 1865

Largest Concentration of Graves: 9 at Maple Grove Cemetery, Sweet Valley, Pennsylvania – Luzerne County

Number of Graves Located: 71

6ᵀᴴ Regiment, Pennsylvania Reserves
(35ᵀᴴ regiment of the line)

Organized: June, 1861

Companies: A – **Columbia** County / B – Snyder County / C – Wayne County
D – Franklin County   E – Montour County / F – Bradford County / G – Dauphin County
H – Tioga County / I – Bradford County / K – Susquehanna County

Company Nicknames:
A – Iron Guards   B – Union Guards   C – Honesdale Guards
D – Washington Rifles   E – Montour Rifles   F – Northern Invincibles
G – J. D. Cameron Infantry   H – Tioga Invincibles   I – Towanda Rifles
K – Susquehanna Volunteers

Corps: Fifth   **Division:** Third   **Brigade:** First

Battles: Drainesville, Second Bull Run, South Mountain, Antietam, Fredericksburg, Gettysburg, Bristoe Station, Mine Run, Wilderness, Spotsylvania, North Anna, and Bethesda Church.

Most Destructive Battle: Fredericksburg (December 13, 1862). The regiment lost 119 men out of about 375 engaged.

Mustered Out of Service: June 14, 1864

Largest Concentration of Graves: 12 at the Rosewood Cemetery, Bloomsburg, Pennsylvania – Columbia County.

Number of Company A Graves Located: 28

Medal of Honor Winners:

<u>Sergeant George W. Mears</u> - *Company A, Rosewood Cemetery, Bloomsburg, Pennsylvania. Was awarded the Medal of Honor for gallantry at the Battle of Gettysburg on July 2, 1863.*

<u>Corporal Chester S. Furman</u> - *Company A, Rosewood Cemetery, Bloomsburg, Pennsylvania. Was awarded the Medal of Honor for gallantry at the Battle of Gettysburg on July 2, 1863.*

7th Regiment, Pennsylvania Reserves
(36th Regiment of the Line)

Organized: June, 1861

Companies: A – Cumberland County / B – Perry County / C – Lebanon County
D – Clinton County / E – Philadelphia / F – **Luzerne** County / G – Philadelphia
H – Cumberland County / I – Lebanon and Berks Counties / K - Philadelphia

Company Nicknames:
A – Carlisle Fencibles   B – Biddle Rifles   C – Iron Artillery
D – Lock Haven Rifle Guards E – Ridgeway Guards   F – **Wyoming Bank Infantry**
G – 2nd Philadelphia Guards H – Cumberland Guards   I – Myerstown Rifles
K – Douglas Guards

Corps: Fifth   **Division:** Third   **Brigade:** Second

Battles: Mechanicsville, Gaines' Mill, New Market Crossroads, Second Bull Run, Turner's Gap, Antietam, Fredericksburg, and the Wilderness.

*Note: The whole regiment, with the exception of Company B, was captured on May 5, 1864 at the Battle of the Wilderness. The remnants of Company B served with the division and were engaged at North Anna River, Spotsylvania, and Bethesda Church.

Most Destructive Battle: Wilderness (May 5, 1864). Most of the regiment, 272 officers and men were cut off and captured by Confederate forces.

Mustered Out of Service: Survivors of Company B were mustered out in June 1864.

Largest Concentration of Graves: 3 at the Pine Hill Cemetery, Shickshinny, Pennsylvania – Luzerne County.

Number of Company F Graves Located: 38

4ᵀᴴ PENNSYLVANIA VOLUNTEER CAVALRY REGIMENT (64ᵀᴴ REGIMENT OF THE LINE)

Organized: September, 1861

Companies: A – Northampton County / B – Allegheny County
C, D – Westmoreland County / E – Allegheny County / F – Lebanon County
G – Allegheny County / H-L – Venango County / M - **Luzerne** County

Company Nicknames:
A – Bethlehem Cavalry   D – Covode Cavalry   L – Oil Creek Cavalry

Corps: Fifth   **Division:** McCall's   **Brigade:** Penna. Reserves
Cavalry   Second   Second

Battles: Seven Days, Antietam, Hedgesville, Kelly's Ford, Rapidan Station, Ely's Ford, Brandy Station, Middleburg, Upperville, Shepherdstown, Jeffersonton, Bristoe Station, Beverly Ford, Yellow Tavern, Haw's Shop, Cold Harbor, Trevilian Station, St. Mary's Church, Jerusalem Plank Road, Hatcher's Run, Dinwiddie Court House, and Farmville.

Most Destructive Battle: Jeffersonton (October 12, 1863). The regiment lost 200 out of about 375 men. Many of these men would later die as prisoners at Andersonville, Georgia.

Mustered Out of Service: July 1, 1865

Largest Concentration of Graves: 9 at the Maplewood Cemetery, Carbondale, Pennsylvania – Lackawanna County.

Number of Graves Located: 65

9ᵀᴴ Pennsylvania Volunteer Cavalry Regiment
(92ᴺᴰ Regiment of the Line)
"The Lochiel Cavalry"

Organized: October, 1861

Companies: A – Perry and Lehigh Counties / B, C – Dauphin County / D – **Luzerne** County
E – Dauphin and Susquehanna Counties / F, G – Lancaster County
H – Cumberland, Dauphin and **Luzerne** Counties / I – Cumberland County
K – Dauphin and **Luzerne** Counties / L – **Luzerne** and Mifflin Counties / M – Blair and Huntingdon Counties

Company Nicknames:
F – Old Guard Mounted Volunteers   G – Greider's Mounted Rangers

Corps: General Stanley's Cavalry Corps   **Division:** First   **Brigade:** First
         General Kilpatrick's Cavalry Corps   Third   First

Battles: Lebanon, Moore's Hill, Tompkinsville, Shelbyville, Perryville, Holston River, Franklin, Spring Hill, Rover, Middletown, Elk River, Cowan, Lafayette, Chickamauga, Dandridge, New Market, Mossy Creek, Fair Garden, Murfreesboro, Woodbury, Lovejoy's Station, Bear Creek, Buckhead Creek, Waynesboro, Blackville, Black Stake's Station, Averysboro, Bentonville, Raleigh, and Morrisville.

*Note: According to Bates' *History of Pennsylvania Volunteers*, the 9ᵗʰ was the last command under General William T. Sherman to fire a shot in the Civil War. Bates also claims that the 9ᵗʰ received the flag of truce from Confederate General Joseph E. Johnston that requested a meeting to discuss surrender.

Most Destructive Battle: Bear Creek (November 22, 1864). The regiment lost 95 out of about 800 men.

Mustered Out of Service: July 18, 1865

Largest Concentration of Graves: 19 at the Hollenback Cemetery, Wilkes-Barre – Luzerne County.

Number of Graves Located: 158

17th Pennsylvania Volunteer Cavalry Regiment

Organized: October, 1862

Companies: A – Beaver County / B – Susquehanna County / C – Lancaster County
D – Bradford County / E – Lebanon County / F – Cumberland County / G – Franklin County / H – Schuylkill County / I – Perry County and Philadelphia / K – **Luzerne** County
L – Chester and Montgomery Counties / M – Wayne County

Company Nicknames:
A – Irwin Cavalry
C – Ephrata Mountain Cavalry
E – Jackson Cavalry

Army: Army of the Potomac   **Corps:** Cavalry Corps   **Division:** First

Battles: Chancellorsville, Brandy Station, Upperville, Gettysburg, Bristoe Station, Mine Run, Yellow Tavern, Wilderness, Spotsylvania, North Anna River, Bethesda Church, Cold Harbor, Trevilian Station, Deep Bottom, Newtown, Front Royal, Kearneysville, Winchester, Gordonsville, White Oak Road, Five Forks, and Farmville.

Most Destructive Battle: Trevilian Station

Mustered Out of Service: August 7, 1865

Largest Concentration of Graves: 8 at the Cathedral Cemetery, Scranton, Pennsylvania – Lackawanna County (formerly Luzerne County).

Number of Graves Located: 83

1ST PENNSYLVANIA LIGHT ARTILLERY (43RD REGIMENT OF THE LINE)

Organized: April, 1861

Batteries: A – Franklin County / B – Lawrence County / C – Philadelphia
D – Philadelphia / E – York / F – Schuylkill, Susquehanna, and Montour Counties
G – Philadelphia and Indiana County / H – Philadelphia and **Luzerne** County
I – most counties throughout the Commonwealth

Battery Nicknames:
B – Mount Jackson Guards   C – Flying Artillery
D – Richmond Artillerists   E – York Artillery

It was common practice in the U.S. military during this period to assign light artillery batteries to different brigades. Therefore, the regiment never acted as one. This was done in order to give advantage to the infantry regiments that the batteries were supporting. Unlike heavy artillery regiments that were quite stationary and suited to fortified positions and sieges, light artillery batteries were horse-drawn and were much more mobile. This ability to move quickly enabled much infantry support in battle.

Battery A
This battery was known as "Easton's Battery" because of its first Captain, Hezekiah Easton. It was engaged at the battles of Dranesville, Beaver Dam Creek, Gaines' Mill, Second Bull Run, South Mountain, Antietam, Fredericksburg, Deep Bottom, Fort Darling, and Petersburg. It served with the I Corps, Army of the Potomac, and the X Corps, Army of the James. It was mustered out of service on July 25, 1865.

Battery B
This battery was known as "Cooper's Battery" because of Captain James Cooper, the first battery commander. It was engaged at the battles of Beaver Dam Creek, Second Bull Run, South Mountain, Antietam, Fredericksburg, Gettysburg, Orange Court House, Spotsylvania Court House, Cold Harbor, Petersburg, and Weldon Railroad. The battery served with the I Corps and V Corps of the Army of the Potomac and fired over 11, 000 rounds of ammunition during its period of service. It was mustered out on June 9, 1865.

Batteries C, D, E, and H

These batteries served together in the Army of the James and can therefore be grouped together. The batteries participated in the fighting at Yorktown, Gaines' Mill, Charles City Crossroads, Malvern Hill, Fredericksburg, Chancellorsville, Gettysburg, Winchester, Cedar Creek, and Drury's Bluff. At various times, these four batteries served with the IV Corps, VI Corps, and the XVIII Corps and were engaged in several different places rendering admirable service.

Battery F

Battery F was known as "Ricketts' Battery" because of its commander, Captain Robert Bruce Ricketts, who is interred at the family cemetery near Lake Ganoga, Pennsylvania. The battery served at the following battles: Dranesville, Bunker Hill, Newtown, Cedar Mountain, Second Bull Run, Antietam, Fredericksburg, Chancellorsville, Gettysburg, Bristoe Station, Wilderness, Cold Harbor, and Petersburg.

At the Battle of Gettysburg, Battery F distinguished itself on the evening of July 2, 1863. It was posted on East Cemetery Hill, in the Union center, and was attacked by an overwhelming force of Confederate Zouaves, known as Hays' Louisiana Tigers. As the screaming Confederates charged the position, the infantrymen assigned to support Ricketts' battery fled in panic, leaving the battery alone. Ricketts' ordered the battery to fire canister, or grapeshot, to decimate the enemy. The rounds had the desired effect and decimated the Confederate force. However, the battery was overrun, but Ricketts' men fought desperately with handspikes, fists, and rocks. A fight for the capture of the battery guidon (small triangular silk flag) ensued, but the men saved the guidon, and the Confederate force was beaten back in confusion. The Wyoming Historical and Geological Society possesses this guidon in its collection and displays it on occasion. According to Bates' *History of Pennsylvania Volunteers*, the Confederate force attacked with about 1,700 men and returned with barely 600.

Following the Petersburg campaign, the battery returned to Harrisburg and was mustered out on June 10, 1865. It had served with the I Corps, II Corps, and XVIII Corps during its service, and is perhaps the most well-known battery of the 1st Light Artillery.

Battery G

This battery was engaged at the battles of Gaines' Mill, Charles City Crossroads, Mechanicsville, Second Bull Run, Fredericksburg, Chancellorsville, Gettysburg (attached to Battery F), Auburn, Bristoe Station, Mine Run, and Washington defenses. It served with the I and II Corps and sustained many casualties. It was mustered out at Philadelphia on June 29, 1865.

Largest Concentration of Graves: There are five each at the Forrest Hill Cemetery, Scranton; Cathedral Cemetery, Scranton; and the Hollenback Cemetery, Wilkes-Barre.

Number of Graves Located: 84

2ND REGIMENT, PENNSYLVANIA HEAVY ARTILLERY
(112TH REGIMENT OF THE LINE)

Organized: October, 1861

Companies: A, B – Philadelphia / C – Philadelphia and Wayne County
D – Philadelphia / E – Philadelphia and Wayne County / F – Philadelphia, Montour, Lycoming, and Columbia Counties / G – Philadelphia / H – Philadelphia and **Carbon** County
I – Philadelphia and Allegheny County / K – Fayette County / L, M – **Luzerne** County

Company Nicknames: None

Corps: Eighteenth **Division:** Second **Brigade:** Second

Battles: Washington fortifications (1861- Spring 1864), Petersburg, Fort Harrison, and Fort Gilmer.

*Note: The regiment took part in the unsuccessful attack on the portion of the Confederate line that was breached when the crater was exploded by the men of the 48th P.V.I. on July 30, 1864.

Most Destructive Battle: Fort Gilmer (September 29, 1864). The regiment lost 237 men.

Mustered Out of Service: January 29, 1866

Largest Concentration of Graves: 18 at the Pittston City Cemetery, Pittston, Pennsylvania - Luzerne County.

Number of Graves Located: 235

3ʳᴰ Regiment, Pennsylvania Heavy Artillery
(152ⁿᴰ regiment of the line)

Organized: May, 1863

Companies: A, B – Philadelphia and New Jersey / C – Philadelphia, Dauphin and Adams Counties / D – Dauphin, Northumberland, Montour, Erie, and York Counties
E – Philadelphia and York County / F, G, H, I – Philadelphia / K – Philadelphia and Berks County / L, M - Philadelphia

Company Nicknames: None

Battles: Heavy artillery regiments were often broken up by companies to perform needed services throughout the army. The 3ʳᵈ was indeed scattered in this way. The headquarters for the regiment was located at Fortress Monroe in the Chesapeake Bay. Batteries A and B served on army gunboats, manning heavy guns on ships patrolling the North Carolina coast. Batteries D, E, G, and M served with the Army of the James during the federal siege of Petersburg, Virginia. Battery F served as prison guards at Camp Hamilton, near Fortress Monroe. Battery I served as headquarters guard for the Army of the James and was present at Appomattox during the surrender of General Robert E. Lee. Battery H was assigned to the Army of the Potomac's Second Cavalry Division to act as light artillery.

Mustered Out of Service: July and November, 1865

Largest Concentration of Graves: 10 at the Cathedral Cemetery, Scranton, Pennsylvania – Lackawanna County (Luzerne County during the Civil War).

Number of Graves Located: 177

BIBLIOGRAPHY

A.   UNPUBLISHED DOCUMENTS AND PAPERS

Personal War Sketches. Post 250, Grand Army of the Republic.
Richards, J. Stuart. Compilation of burial records of Schuylkill County men in the Civil War. Schuylkill County Historical Society, 1999.
Throne, Walter. Compilation of burial records of Hazleton men in the Civil War. Hazleton Historical Society, 1995.
U.S. Army service and pension records. United States National Archives, Washington D.C.
Veteran burial records. Carbon County Veterans Affairs Division, Jim Thorpe, PA.
Veteran burial records, Grand Army of the Republic. Tamaqua Historical Society, Tamaqua, PA.
Veteran burial records. Luzerne County Veterans Affairs Division, Wilkes-Barre, PA

B.   PUBLISHED SOURCES

Bates, Samuel P. History of Pennsylvania Volunteers. 2nd edition. Wilmington North Carolina: Broadfoot Publishing Company, 1994.
Beyer, W.F. and Keydel, O.F., ed. Deeds of Valor. 2nd edition. Stamford, Connecticut: Longmeadow Press, 1992.
Bradsby, H.C. History of Luzerne County with Biographical Selections. Chicago, Illinois: S.B. Nelson and Co., 1893.
Faust, Patricia, ed. Historical Times Illustrated Encyclopedia of the Civil War. New York, N.Y.: Harper Collins Publishing Company, 1991.
Fox, William F. Regimental Losses in the American Civil War. 2nd edition. Dayton, Ohio: Morningside Bookshop, 1985.
Freeze, J.G. The History of Columbia County. Bloomsburg, Pennsylvania, 1883.
Harvey, Oscar J. A History of Wilkes Barre and Luzerne County. Wilkes Barre, Pennsylvania: Oscar J. Harvey, 1909.
Hayden, Horace E. Genealogical and Family History of the Wyoming and Lackawanna Valleys. Vol. 2. New York and Chicago: Lewis Publishing Co., 1906.
Hitchcock, Frederick L. History of Scranton and Its People. New York, N.Y.: Lewis Historical Publishing Co., 1914.

Johnson, F.C., ed. <u>The Historical Record</u>. Wilkes-Barre, Pennsylvania: Johnson Publishing, 1890-3.

Laciar, J.D. <u>Patriotism of Carbon County, Pennsylvania</u>. Mauch Chunk, Pennsylvania, 1867.

Mott, Smith B. <u>The Campaigns of the Fifty Second Regiment Pennsylvania Volunteer Infantry</u>. Philadelphia, Pennsylvania: J.B. Lippincott Co., 1911.

Nicholson, John P., ed. <u>Pennsylvania at Gettysburg</u>. Harrisburg, Pennsylvania: Commonwealth of Pennsylvania, 1904.

Sauers, Richard A. <u>Advance the Colors! Pennsylvania Civil War Battle Flags</u>. Harrisburg, Pennsylvania: Capitol Preservation Committee, 1987.

Thompson, Katherine F. <u>Chapter and Verse: Annotated Diaries of Asa Lansford Foster</u>. Wilmington, Delaware: Thompson Publications, 1992.

Tomasak, Peter, ed. <u>Avery Harris Civil War Journal</u>. Luzerne, Pennsylvania: Luzerne National Bank, 2000.

C. NEWSPAPERS AND PERIODICALS

Wilkes-Barre Record
Scranton Times
Times Leader

Gone But Not Forgotten | *Civil War Veterans of Northeastern Pennsylvania*

MEMORIAL TO CAPTAIN CHARLES H. FLAGG, CO. K, 142ND PENNSYLVANIA VOLUNTEER INFANTRY,
KILLED IN ACTION AT GETTYSBURG ON JULY 3, 1863 - HOLLENBACK CEMETERY, WILKES-BARRE, PENNSYLVANIA
CREDIT: KRISTEN LINDBUCHLER PHOTO